THEOLOGY FROM EXILE:
Commentary on the Revised Common
Lectionary for an Emerging Christianity

The Year of Luke

Sea Raven, D.Min.

Cover design by Jinjer Stanton.

ISBN-13: 978-1481070591

Table of Contents

ACKNOWLEDGMENTS

We get by with a little help from our friends. Special thanks to George Crossman, for initial editing and challenging theological questions, and Carol B. Singer for eagle-eyed copyediting. Special thanks to Professor Amy-Jill Levine for taking precious time for a serious critique. None of this would have even begun without the inspiration of Rev. Dr. Matthew Fox, and the scholars of the Jesus Seminar.

Introduction
Theology from Exile

This book is the first in a series of commentaries on biblical scripture that follows the three-year cycle of Christian liturgical readings found in the *Revised Common Lectionary[1]* (RCL). Appendix One contains reimagined rituals of Holy Communion that reflect an invitation to commit to a new partnership with a non-theistic, "kenotic God"[2] in the ongoing salvation work of non-violent, distributive, justice-compassion. Appendix Two is a Bible study for Holy Week that explores in depth the meaning of *kenosis*. This project is grounded in the paradigm-shifting biblical scholarship of Karen Armstrong, Marcus J. Borg, John Dominic Crossan, Robert Funk, and Amy-Jill Levine, as well as the transformative work of Rev. Dr. Matthew Fox, whose theology of Creation Spirituality has reclaimed Catholic mysticism for post-modern cosmology.

Four Questions for the Apocalypse

The underlying framework for the commentaries is a series of four questions.

1) What is the nature of God? Violent or non-violent?
2) What is the nature of Jesus's message? Inclusive or exclusive?
3) What is faith? Literal belief, or trust in God's realm of distributive justice- compassion?
4) What is deliverance? Salvation from hell or liberation from injustice?

These questions address what might be seen as apocalyptic times for humanity on Planet Earth. The twenty-first century – much like the first century – finds human social structures embroiled in political, social, spiritual, and theological issues that demand serious consideration of the answers to these questions. Unlike the first century, twenty-first century humanity is also confronted with the distinct possibility of a holocaust that is not

---

[1]*Consultation on Common Texts, Revised Common Lectionary*, Nashville: Abingdon Press, 1992.

[2]Crossan and Reed, *In Search of Paul*, 288ff.

confined to individuals, tribes, or nations, but threatens the very existence of planetary life as humanity has known it for 100,000 years.

Two possible choices arise from the answers to these four questions.

If the answers are: Violent, Exclusive, Literal Belief, and Salvation from Hell, then the context for personal, social, and political life is Empire, and the theology of Empire: Piety, War, Victory, Peace.[3] "Empire" is normally defined in political and historical terms such as the Roman Empire, or the Persian Empire. John Dominic Crossan has developed the concept of Empire as a cultural framework – even a theology – that includes religious unity (piety); war (that defends or expands political power); victory (ensuring future security); and peace (the rule of imperial law and cultural hegemony). Further, Crossan suggests that Empire may be the inevitable outcome of normal human attempts at social organization (the "normalcy of civilization"). However, Crossan is quite clear that the "normalcy of civilization" is not due to human nature – hence the possibility (and continuing hope) for choosing different answers to the four questions proposed.

If the answers to the four questions are: Nonviolent, Inclusive, Trust, and Liberation, then the context for personal, social, and political life is participation in the ongoing work – the struggle – for distributive justice-compassion, in Covenant. *Distributive* justice-compassion is here defined as radical fairness, which is in direct opposition to the *retributive* "justice" of normal social systems. Instead of payback and revenge, distributive justice-compassion offers grace and radical fairness. The Covenant to participate in establishing such a paradigm is with a non-theistic, *kenotic* god, a force which – in John Dominic Crossan's words – "is the beating heart of the Universe, whose presence is justice and life, and whose absence is injustice and death."[4] The Covenant then reflects the inclusive peaceable kingdom described by the Old Testament prophets, in which "they will not hurt or destroy in all my holy mountain."[5]

---

[3]Ibid.

[4]Ibid., 291.

[5]Isaiah 11:9a

Christianity has been in danger of diverting into false paths from the beginning. One of those false paths, which is all too easily found in John's Gospel, opposes Christian "enlightenment" to the "darkness" of Jewish tradition. Another is the path that leads to collaboration with political empire. The Four Horsemen of the Apocalypse – War, Famine, Disease, and Death – galloping down the ages out of the Revelation of John – have brought humanity to the brink of extinction in the twenty-first century. We continue to terrorize ourselves with their seeming inevitability. Whether or not that metaphor is the one that prevails depends upon how humanity (not just Christians) ultimately answers the questions. The choice in these commentaries is clear.

John Shelby Spong has called for a profound change in the practice of Christianity that can carry us both back to its roots, and forward into a new Christianity relevant to life in the third millennium:

> I see in this moment of Christian history a new vocation . . . to legitimize the questions, the probings, and, in whatever form, the faith of the *believer in exile*. . . . [A] conversation and a dialogue must be opened with those who cannot any longer give their assent to those premodern theological concepts that continue to mark the life of our increasingly irrelevant ecclesiastical institution. . . . [T]he time has come for the Church to invite its people into a frightening journey into the mystery of God and to stop proclaiming that somehow the truth of God is still bound by either our literal scriptures or our literal creeds.[6]

This series, "Theology from Exile," applies Spong's concept to anyone who cannot accept orthodox Christian belief systems, yet is drawn to the social justice mandate found in such collections of Jesus's teachings as the Sermon on the Mount. The commentaries are intended to address the "so what" question,

---

[6]Spong, *Why Christianity Must Change*, 21.

implied by the continuing, ground-breaking work of the Westar Institute's Jesus Seminar scholars and others who are concerned with the role of Christianity, and religion in general, in the twenty-first century. Now that we have some sense of what the historical Jesus (a first-century Galilean Jew speaking to other Jews) actually said, taught, and did, so what? What does our Christian scriptural tradition mean now? Can we rely on the canon? What does this knowledge do to (or for) Christian liturgy – specifically, such defining rituals as Baptism and Holy Communion?

In his book, *Jesus: Uncovering the Life, Teachings, and Relevance of a Religious Revolutionary,* Marcus J. Borg contrasts doctrinal Christianity with an "emerging paradigm" that has been "the dominant understanding in divinity schools and seminaries of mainline churches" for most of the twentieth century. The problem is, that "emerging paradigm" has largely remained behind closed seminary classroom doors, and has not made it into the minds of the people occupying the pews in church on Sunday morning. These commentaries and accompanying liturgies are intended to provide courage to clergy and enlightenment to lay leadership in the sometimes "frightening journey" described by Spong, to integrate personal spirituality with twenty-first century cosmological realities. This series is a contribution to that dialogue for clergy, and a catalyst for progressive, lay-led Bible study groups.

Many of these commentaries contain a shorthand term that illustrates the frustration of worship leaders when confronted with the seeming unrelatedness of the liturgical readings proposed by the RCL. A clergy friend (now retired) describes the cherry-picking among the various portions of scripture as having been put together by "drunken elves." The RCL provides its own clues as to how and/or why certain passages from the Old Testament are paired with certain passages from the New. The most recent version (1992) certainly is its own testimony to the hard work of coming up with a three-year cycle of "common texts" that Catholics and mainline Protestants can use throughout the Christian liturgical year of Sundays, Holy Days, Feast Days, and Seasons.

But as these commentaries point out, all too often the Old Testament readings are snipped out of context in order to support

Christian messianic claims. This process functions to the detriment of Jewish wisdom, and it thereby robs Christianity of a rich source for understanding the message of Jesus himself. Worse, such selectivity legitimizes Christian hegemony, supersessionism, and ultimately anti-Semitism. While "the Elves" may seem to be subject to quite a bit of abuse here, no individual disrespect is intended. In addition, it is by no means an insult to the nobility of the Elven Race (as described by J.R.R. Tolkien) who long ago abandoned Middle Earth to its fate – a caution to those who use proof-texting to justify compliance with Empire.

Season of Advent and Christmas

Apocalypse Now – First Sunday in Advent

Jeremiah 33:14-16; 1ˢᵗ Thessalonians 3:9-13; Luke 21:25-36

The first Sunday in Advent, which begins Year C in the Common Lectionary, is filled with apocalypticism. God at last is going to act, says Jeremiah, and God will act again, says Luke's militant Jesus – presumably because God didn't get the job done the first time, unless of course you are a "dispensationalist," who believes that the entire Bible is the coherent, linearly-timed word of God, to be applied literally to the conditions we find ourselves in today.

It's very curious that Jesus seems to be talking about himself coming again. He sounds like the over-committed twenty-first century soccer mom who's so busy she meets herself coming and going. And why couldn't God get it done within Jesus' lifetime? Serious minds stumble over these questions.

Considering the Lukan readings for Advent, it appears the creators of the Revised Common Lectionary are cherry-picking scripture to prove a point: starting from the apocalypticism of Luke 21, then jumping back to Luke 3, and finally turning to Luke 1 and 2 for Christmas Eve and Christmas Day. Interpreted in the orthodox way, of course, all this frogging around is to prove that Jesus is the One who will finally bring God's Justice to fruition in this wicked world – even if he has to rise from the dead and come back again to finish the job. The brief verses from Paul's first letter to the Thessalonians for the first Sunday are a prayer that God will strengthen our hearts so that when the Lord comes (again), we will be blameless. Believers are off the hook. There is nothing to do except go shopping.

"The days are surely coming," Jeremiah says in the name of God, "when I will fulfill the promise I made to the house of Israel and the house of Judah. . . ." God promises the exiled Jews in Babylon that the lineage of the great king David will be restored to the throne in Israel, and God's distributive justice will be reestablished. Jeremiah speaks to the people in exile. Luke writes to the followers of Jesus, probably both Jewish and non-Jewish, in the diaspora after the destruction of the Jerusalem temple. Both peoples are looking at apocalypse: the end of life as they knew it, and both are claiming that God is just, and the world belongs to God; therefore, the world has to be just, and if it isn't, God will do something to make it so.

It's much easier and certainly more assuring to just suspend disbelief. Signing on to the program Jesus offers – that is, participating in the Kingdom of God and in opposition to the Empire – means more than hands-on acts for justice and peace. Participating in the Kingdom here and now may have more meaning than waiting for eternal life. Certainly Jesus's death is an example of this, however his death is interpreted. But even more important is authentic encounter with the other, whether friend or enemy, oppressor or oppressed, rich or poor.

Two examples come to mind. The first, from the war in El Salvador in the 1980s to early-'90s, from unpublished testimony of Jennifer Jean Casolo at the American University, Washington, DC, January 24, 1990:

> "Suffering," I said, "is not the worst thing you can do. Being cruel is a lot worse." And I told [the interrogator] what I just told you. . . . And I said, "Thank you. I understand now that my life is not my own. In two years I have known this lesson – that what God requires of us is to transcend ourselves for those we love. . . . And I have never been able to live it until this one moment, I understand. And I understand the hope of your people. Thank you. You have freed me." And he wrote my confession: Jennifer, age, name, all that information – does not know anything about the weapons. She is innocent. She has the right to have a lawyer, etc., etc. He let me read it, and I signed it. . . . Hope. That each one of us can live a life that proclaims life . [And] we believe. We believe because we have witnessed people who have claimed their own dignity. No matter what the cost. And you know that they can put up with anything, with everything. . . . What the Salvadorans want isn't difficult . . . negotiated settlement to the war. That can only be achieved

by strengthening efforts of peace and life, not strengthening efforts of war.

The second is from the November-December 2006 issue of *Sojourners* magazine. On November 26, 2005, four members of the Christian Peacemaker Teams in Iraq – Tom Fox, James Loney, Norman Kember, and Harmeet Singh Sooden – were taken captive at gunpoint in Baghdad. Tom Fox was ultimately murdered. In "118 Days: How I survived captivity in Iraq,"[7] Loney describes his relationship with his fellow prisoners:

> Each day, each hour, each minute I was confronted with a choice: withdraw, clench my heart into a fist, and conserve my widow's mite of emotional energy or open my heart, inhabit the moment, be generous with acceptance and conversation and listening. Sometimes, the misery of captivity would dissolve into sharing about our lives: games of Wheel of Fortune, riddles, discussions about bad movies or strategies for unlearning racism, heated Quaker, Baptist, and Catholic Bible exegesis. . . . This, I began to see, is what it means to be born again. The present moment [is] the birth canal of incarnation.

What is apocalypse now? Unlike being carried off into exile by sixth century B.C.E. agents of empire or witnessing the destruction of the temple in first century C.E. Jerusalem, latter-day apocalypse is a process that renews itself with every scientific discovery, whether it is of viruses, new galaxies, or stem cell research. Twenty-first century people must either suspend disbelief in an interventionist God, or embrace the desolation encountered in inner and outer space when religious literalism breaks down in the presence of experience. Maybe this is the real meaning of the flaming swords blocking any hope of return to Eden.

---

[7]Loney, "118 Days," 12.

Going for Baruch: Second Sunday in Advent

Baruch 5:1-9; Malachi 3:1-4; Luke 1:68-79;
Philippians 1:3-11; Luke 3:1-6

From the Babylonian exile the persona named Baruch writes a letter to Jerusalem: "Arise, O Jerusalem, stand upon the height; look toward the east, and see your children gathered from west and east at the word of the Holy One, rejoicing that God has remembered them. For they went out from you on foot, led away by their enemies; but God will bring them back to you, carried in glory, as on a royal throne. For God has ordered that every high mountain and the everlasting hills be made low and the valleys filled up, to make level ground, so that Israel may walk safely in the glory of God. The woods and every fragrant tree have shaded Israel at God's command. For God will lead Israel with joy, in the light of his glory, with the mercy and righteousness that come from him."

And Luke begins his great pageant of the story of Jesus with the birth of John the Baptist – the signal that God's justice was going to come down hard, fast, and soon upon the oppressors of the people in their own land.

These are precious readings, telling the story of the birth of the one Christians believe to be the Messiah, the Savior, the Liberator, who would cause God's justice/compassion to at last hold sway. God's whole creation was for the purpose of this anointed one's birth, who would reconcile fallen humanity with God, and return those exiled from God's Eden.

For most Christians – as well as non-Christians – the story has not changed. But for some, the exile is not only from God's Kingdom, it is from the Church that misinterpreted the meaning of the story from the beginning, and has been either unable or unwilling to reinterpret the story as human understanding and consciousness have evolved.

Who are the exiles from the Church of Jesus Christ today? Those who have left the interventionist God of childhood far behind, who have set down roots in a latter-day Babylon, where new understandings about who Jesus was and what Jesus said reconstruct and transform the faith. These exiles have been carried off to the sacred equilibrium of the natural world, find salvation in the awesome nature of the cosmos, and divinity revealed in all acts of compassionate justice. These exiles reject the idea of a second coming of Jesus as written in the New Testament, and are appalled by the notion that these legends are the foundation of the foreign policy of the most militarily, politically, and economically powerful nation on earth.

Suppose one of these exiles were to write a letter today, much as Baruch wrote from Babylon in the sixth century B.C.E., or the Apostle Paul wrote to the community in Philippi? To whom would such a letter be written? Many people today have been left behind in an occupied spiritual Jerusalem, taken over by fearful literalists, and by fundamentalists, many of whom have sold out to the prevailing corporate and commercial powers aligned with today's imperial rulers. They see the hypocrisy and the injustice of the occupiers, and have given up. To the question of whether Jesus's teachings apply in any way to twenty-first century life, they say no. And yet they long for the story to have meaning – especially at Christmas. And so they suspend disbelief, listen to Handel's Messiah, sing the carols, and insist that the pageant set forth in Luke's Gospel be read from the King James version of the Bible so they can feel however briefly that long lost childhood "Christmas spirit."

In the spirit of Baruch, whose own story is lost in the legends of antiquity, I offer this memorandum to the aliens and exiles in Christ:

Do not give up. Jesus's life and the way of life he taught are more relevant than ever, not because he will personally save you from physical death, or the flames of some medieval hell, but because the justice-compassion he taught will save humankind from self-destruction. If you succumb to despair, the desperate win. We warned of global warming and lost our good name; we defended human rights and lost our lives; we taught our children to think for themselves, and they were expelled from school; we reported corporate malfeasance and government corruption and we lost our jobs. But all that is over with now if you will go out to the mountaintops that have not yet been removed in the futile search for non-renewable sources of energy and watch the earth turn toward the new day. All Jesus asks is that we participate in

God's justice-compassion. In the words of the wisdom of this age, we are the ones we have been waiting for.

Who is the One that is Coming?
Third Sunday in Advent

Luke 3:7-18; Zephaniah 3:14-20; Isaiah 12:2-6;
Philippians 4:4-7

These readings for the third Sunday in Advent provide two views of the nature of God: violent and nonviolent. If God is just, and the world belongs to God, but the world is not just, then will God rectify the situation with violence – retributive consequences – or nonviolence – compassionate fairness?

John the Baptist is clearly on the side of violence: "Even now the ax is lying at the root of the trees; every tree therefore that does not bear good fruit is cut down and thrown into the fire . . . one who is more powerful than I is coming. . . ." He blasts his hearers, calls them a nest of snakes, says don't hide behind the fact that you are the children of Abraham. God is perfectly capable of raising up new children of Abraham out of the very stones, so he doesn't need you. Then finally, when he has terrorized the crowds into asking what they can possibly do to save themselves from God's wrath, the Baptizer suggests justice: "Whoever has two coats must share them with anyone who has none; and whoever has food must do likewise." He tells the tax collectors not to cheat, the military not to extort money, and that all be satisfied with their wages.

John is not preaching only to the oppressed poor. He is preaching to those who have two coats, to the rich tax collectors, and to members of the ruling elite, who extort payment from everyone with threats and false accusations. And they love it – especially the part where John says he's not the messiah. The messiah who is coming will bring even more violence down upon the heads of those who do not change their ways. "His winnowing fork is in his hand, to clear his threshing floor and to gather the wheat into his granary; but the chaff he will burn with unquenchable fire." It's cathartic. We who repent will be saved, and the bad guys will definitely pay.

We've heard all this before – every three years, in fact, when the lectionary gets around to Year C. Most of us think we are off the hook. "Bear fruits worthy of repentance," says John. And we

15

do. We bundle up our unwanted clothing and call Purple Heart to come and get it. We give money to the church soup kitchen project, and we may even go help serve turkey to the homeless, or do a stint at a shelter for a few hours during the holidays. So what do we have to repent or feel regret or shame about? We certainly don't extort money from anyone. So, "Come O come, Emmanuel," we sing, "and ransom captive Israel." It is a military metaphor of forced exile. The Baptizer's violent God punishes the people with political and military oppression for turning away from God's law, and requires a price to be paid before justice and peace can be restored.

Likewise, the readings from the prophets Zephaniah and Isaiah promise violent deliverance for the exiled people of Israel, who shall return home once their enemies have been thoroughly vanquished. Isaiah promises a great king from the lineage of David, who will restore the people to their own land. "You will say in that day: I will give thanks to you, O Lord, for though you were angry with me, your anger turned away, and you comforted me. . . . With joy you will draw water from the wells of salvation. And you will say in that day: give thanks to the Lord, call on his name; make known his deeds among the nations. . . . Shout aloud and sing for joy, O royal Zion, for great in your midst is the Holy One of Israel." Zephaniah prophesies judgment against Jerusalem as well as the ones carried off into exile. God says, "In the fire of my passion all the earth shall be consumed." Then and only then will the people be restored and no longer need to be afraid. "The Lord has taken away the judgments against you, he has turned away your enemies. . . . On that day it shall be said to Jerusalem: Do not fear, O Zion; The Lord your God is in your midst; . . . At that time I will bring you home. . . . I will make you renowned and praised among all the peoples of the earth when I restore your fortunes before your eyes, says the Lord."

How a people define their gods determines their definition of justice. If god is violent, uncompromising, requiring payment (an eye for an eye), then justice will be retributive, and revenge or self-interest (what's in it for me?) will be what governs interactions between people. The law of the land in the United States is that one is innocent of wrongdoing until proven guilty. Yet the prevailing attitude among the people toward those accused or even suspected is the opposite. The ones who have borne bad fruit – a local drug dealer or bank robber, or Saddam Hussein, or the so-called "enemy combatants" plucked off the battlefields in Afghanistan and Iraq – are either on trial for their lives, or are safely shut up in prisons.

Traditional Christian dogma claims Jesus's life as the price for salvation, which usually means winning eternity in heaven instead of hell. But Jesus, whom John the Baptist recognized as the messiah, early in his ministry rejected John's retributive apocalypticism and John's violent God. Jesus invited his followers to look within to find the Kingdom of God, and to open eyes and ears and choose to participate in that kingdom now, not in some heaven at the end of time. In Philippians 4:4-7, Paul makes it clear that neither Jesus nor Jesus's God is violent. He advises the followers of Jesus way to "Let your gentleness be known to everyone. The Lord is near. Do not worry about anything, but in everything by prayer and supplication with thanksgiving let your requests be made known to God. And the peace of God which surpasses all understanding will guard your hearts and your minds in Christ Jesus."

The Christian Science Monitor of Monday, December 11, 2006, reported that on Friday, December 8, in a public hearing in London, the three surviving members of the Christian Peacemaker Team who had been held captive in Iraq from November 2005 through March 2006 said they did not want "punitive" justice for their suspected captors. James Loney said:

> Justice is about restoring relationships that have been broken. We are very, very concerned about the death penalty. It would be the worst possible outcome for us if they were to be sentenced to death. To lock them up and throw away the key is not justice. Punishment comes from the same mind-set that is behind the escalating spiral of violence that we see in Iraq that is being fueled by the governments in Washington and London. If they are punishing them on my behalf, that doesn't do anything for me.

The story goes on to report that if the three men do not testify against their captors, either by identifying the suspects in

17

photographs or by giving video evidence, the case could unravel. Loney says: "We were told there would be a possibility that they could walk away from this if we don't testify. Not to excuse what they were doing, but there was a rationale for it. They saw themselves being part of a fight to defend their country."

This extraordinary stand for compassion could result in no justice in a retributive system. In the Kingdom of God, however, where the rain falls on the just and the unjust, understanding the other, suffering with the other, restores relationship, and brings reconciliation and true peace. What is most important to Mr. Loney is to return to Iraq and meet with his former captors, to talk with them about what they did and what it meant to them then, and what it means to them now.

Those who love their enemies have no enemies. Perhaps even the crazed Baptizer, screaming out his frustration at the edge of town, realized that nonviolence is more powerful than violence, and that the fruits of his work didn't even qualify him to be a slave to God's anointed one. "I baptize you with water," John says, "but one who is more powerful than I is coming; [and] I am not worthy to untie the thong of his sandals."

Magnificat: Fourth Sunday in Advent

Luke 1:39-55; John 1:1-14

It's no accident that the organizers of the early Christian church claimed the Winter Solstice as the time for the birth of the Christ. If Jesus had been born in Tierra del Fuego, perhaps the inhabitants of the Northern Hemisphere would be the ones obliged at high summer to bend the metaphors of the coming of light. But Earth's geography and the pattern of human civilization dictated otherwise. North of the Equator, December is the darkest time, especially on those days when the moon rises and sets with the sun, and will not be seen again until two or three days later, after the sun has made its own turn, and the light begins to strengthen again. The cosmology behind the tradition matches perfectly the experience of premodern, pre-enlightenment people. The powers of death and darkness are defeated by the rebirth of the sun, and the human birth of the Son of God, the Light of the World, the *Sun* of God.

Postmodern, post-enlightenment people cannot reconcile a changing, developing, evolving postmodern, post-enlightenment cosmology with traditional religious belief. We must allow literal belief to become metaphor that can continue to give meaning to experience. Otherwise, we end up with an intolerable spiritual schizophrenia, in which what we hear preached at us has no relevance to our lives, and we are condemned to purposeless exile.

The liturgist is free to pick and choose among the selections from the RCL for the Fourth Sunday in Advent, Christmas Eve, and Christmas Day. These are the traditional readings for the season of Christmas, which are divided among "Propers" I, II, and III. However, the accompanying explanatory note declares, "[i]f Proper III is not used on Christmas Day, it should be used at some service during the Christmas cycle because of the significance of John's prologue." The Prologue to the Gospel of John (John 1:1-14) is the quintessential reworking of the creation story in Genesis 1. From the birth of Jesus on, the New Testament supersedes the Old, according to traditional dogma. It is clear from nearly every translation of these passages that the "Word" of God is Jesus the Christ. "He was in the world, and the world came into being

19

through him; yet the world did not know him. . . . And the Word became flesh and lived among us, and we have seen his glory, the glory as of a father's only son."

Two sources for postmodern Christians seeking meaningful Christian metaphor are the work of the Westar Institute (popularly known as The Jesus Seminar) and the work of Rev. Dr. Matthew Fox. In 1995, Robert W. Funk and The Jesus Seminar published *The Five Gospels: The Search for the Authentic Words of Jesus.* Because the purpose of the translation was to highlight what their research indicated were truly most likely the actual words spoken by Jesus, the scholars provide no interpretation of their translation of the Prologue. Perhaps none is needed:

> In the beginning there was the divine word and wisdom. The divine word and wisdom was there with God, and it was what God was. It was there with God from the beginning. Everything came to be by means of it; nothing that exists came to be without its agency. In it was life, and this life was the light of humanity. Light was shining in darkness, and darkness did not master it.
>
> There appeared a man sent from God named John. He came to testify – to testify to the light – so everyone would believe through him. He was not the light; he came only to attest to the light.
>
> Genuine light – the kind that provides light for everyone – was coming into the world. Although it was in the world, and the world came about through its agency, the world did not recognize it. It came to its own place, but its own people were not receptive to it. But to all who did embrace it, to those who believed in it, it gave the right to become children of God. They were not born from sexual union, not from physical desire, and not from male willfulness: they were born of God.
>
> The divine word and wisdom became human and made itself at home among us. We have seen its majesty, majesty appropriate to a Father's only son, brimming with generosity and truth.

Referring to God's word, wisdom, and light as "it" removes the anthropomorphism that has plagued the interpretations of the meaning of Jesus's life and teachings since the middle of the 1st century. When the Light is not personified as the "only son of God" who requires belief, it is an inclusive metaphor. Anyone who recognizes the word and wisdom – the light – of God has the right to become children of God – not physical, literal children, but recognized as part of God, born of God. When the divine word and wisdom becomes human, and at home among us, it manifests as unlimited, abundant generosity and truth.

In *Sins of the Spirit, Blessings of the Flesh*, Matthew Fox describes the Eucharist – the defining ritual of Christianity:

> The Eucharist is about the universe loving us unconditionally still one more time and giving itself to us in the most intimate way (as food and drink). Interconnectivity is the heart of the Eucharistic experience: God and humanity coming together, God and flesh, the flesh of wheat, wine, sunshine, soil, water, human ingenuity, stars, supernovas, galaxies, storms, fireballs – every Eucharist has a 15-billion-year sacred story that renders it holy. The Eucharist is heart food from the cosmos – the "mystical body of Christ" and the Cosmic Christ or Buddha nature found in all beings in the universe – to us. Christ is the light of the world, which we now know is made only of light. Flesh is light and light is flesh. We eat, drink, sleep, breathe, and love that light. The Eucharist is also our hearts expanding and responding generously: "Yes, we will." We will carry on the heart-work called compassion, the work of the cosmos itself.[8]

Here is a postmodern, post-enlightenment metaphor that reflects the Cosmology of the twenty-first century. This "Cosmic Christ" does not spring from one physical life in the unprovable past. This Cosmic Christ is expressed and experienced in the very nature of the universe itself. This generosity, this justice-compassion, is

---

[8]Fox, *Sins of the Spirit,* 270-271.

what Mary sings about in Luke's Magnificat (Luke 1:39-55). "For the Mighty One . . . has brought down the powerful from their thrones, and lifted up the lowly; he has filled the hungry with good things, and sent the rich away empty." Mary's song is of liberation, of God's justice-compassion at last established "according to the promise he made to our ancestors, to Abraham and to his descendants forever." We sing about the little town of Bethlehem, where Jesus was born. "O come to us, abide with us, our Lord Emmanuel." God's justice-compassion comes, manifests, is incarnated in any and all who choose to participate in it.

A Different Bethlehem?
Christmas Propers I, II, III

Luke 2:1-20, 41-52; Colossians 3:12-17; Revelation 21:1-6a

In 2006, according to wire service reports, and a *Christian Science Monitor* story by Amelia Thomas,[9] the "security wall" constructed by the Israeli government separating the Palestinian West Bank from Israel reduced the Christmas tourist trade in Bethlehem from five thousand visitors per day to fifty. Businesses were closed, hours were curtailed. The only way in was through a checkpoint that blocked the centuries-old pilgrimage route from Jerusalem.

According to Amelia Thomas's story, Aviram Oshri, an archaeologist with the Israeli Antiquities Authority, claimed that the Bethlehem mentioned in the Bible was actually another one, near Nazareth, and in Israel, not Palestine. In fact, the Israeli Antiquities Authority has just as much credibility as anyone. Most of the places of pilgrimage were chosen by conquering Romans and crusading Europeans, who rode through the area and appropriated traditional sites that had been sacred to the people for thousands of years. For example, the Church of the Nativity is built over a much earlier shrine to the Greek god Adonis.

Sacred sites have lives of their own. For reasons that are not understood by our postmodern insistence on scientifically verifiable fact, crossroads, springs, underground waterways, nexus points with the sun at solstice or equinox evoke numinous experiences that provide meaning, purpose, beauty, and order to the chaotic universe within which humanity survives. The accumulated experience of two millennia of Christian devotion to the holy land carries that same spiritual power – power enhanced and expressed in music: Handel's *Messiah*; the Bach *Christmas Oratorio*; thousands of songs, tunes, poems from an astounding diversity of cultures worldwide, creating the reality of the hillside, the grotto, the stable, the inn. Legend and pageant have become inseparably blended with imagined history. For Christians, to travel to these sites is to touch hope. But hope for what? Peace on

---

[9]Lampman, "Mixing prophecy and politics."

Earth? Goodwill toward men? Hope that at the end of this life the pilgrim will go to heaven rather than hell?

We look around at the world that is supposed to belong to a just God, and we see war, famine, disease, and death. Where is the new Jerusalem revealed to John of Patmos? The governors of the Planet are determined to follow the imperial imperative: piety, war, victory, peace. From the Horn of Africa to the Isthmus of Panama, men – and they are mostly men – happily trade their people's welfare for their own political power. The U.S. economy teeters on the edge of believable strength. If you have stocks and mutual funds, the economy is very very good. If you need two incomes to make ends meet, the economy tanked three years ago. Saddam Hussein, condemned to death for genocide and torture, claims martyrdom and a direct, nonstop trip to paradise. Traditional Christian dogma proclaims Jesus as the Christ, King of Kings, Lord of Lords, whose Kingdom is forever. He comes not to bring peace, but a sword. "Those who conquer will inherit these things," Jesus says to John of Patmos, "and I will be their God and they will be my children. But as for the cowardly, the faithless, the polluted, the murderers, the fornicators, the sorcerers, the idolaters, and all liars, their place will be in the lake that burns with fire and sulfur, which is the second death." John's God is a violent God. Not one violent death, but two for the losers. Above the gap in the concrete wall through which visitors may move into Bethlehem after passport checks, the Israeli Tourist Board message reads, "Go in Peace." This is imperial cynicism.

Does it really matter where Jesus was born, or what hillside the shepherds were on when the angel visited? In the reading from Luke, Jesus asks his parents why they were searching for him. "Did you not know that I must be in my Father's house?" Why should twenty-first century Christians search for Jesus in the traditional places? Perhaps he was never there. The reading from the Revelation of John declares a new Jerusalem; why not a different Bethlehem? Maybe we need a new Bethlehem, one not compromised by Empire, injustice, and crass commercialism. So long as Christians (or anyone) rely on violent Empire to bring peace on earth, there will be none. Jesus offers covenant, nonviolence, justice-compassion, and peace to all who choose to participate in God's Kingdom. Colossians was probably not written by Paul, but the reading for the first Sunday after Christmas reflects Paul's interpretation of Jesus's message: "Above all, clothe yourselves with love . . . and let the peace of Christ rule in your hearts . . . ."

Epiphany

The Epiphany of the Lord

Isaiah 60:1-6; Psalm 72:1-7, 10-14; Ephesians 3:1-12;
Matthew 2:1-12

The predominant metaphor of the Epiphany of the Lord is of royal power and political triumph not only for the nation of Israel, but for the followers of God's Messiah. "Arise, shine, for your light has come," sings Isaiah. "Nations shall come to your light, and kings to the brightness of your dawn." Psalm 72 is a coronation anthem. The writer of Ephesians declares that through the "church" – the organized network of believers – "the wisdom of God . . . might now be made known to the rulers and authorities" in opposition to it. The birth of the royal child in Matthew's famous adventure of the three wise men – kings, sages from the East – presents a direct threat to Herod, the Roman-appointed ruling power in Palestine.

The stage is set for revolution. What happened?

By the end of the first century, fifty to seventy years after the birth of Jesus, without the benefit of the most rudimentary of communication technologies, the fledgling organization of the descendants of the followers of Jesus had already been diverted from Jesus's original teachings, and a new organized religion had already been created and aligned with the principalities and powers of the Roman world. Somehow, the homogenizing process of human institutionalization manages to derail even the best laid plans of God himself. John Dominic Crossan calls it "the normalcy of civilization." Crossan is very clear that he is not talking about human nature, but the inevitable progression toward self-selecting hierarchies, leading to power struggles, and systemic injustice.

Probably the greatest misinterpretation of Jesus's message was to "dumb it down" from an invitation to participate in systemic distributive justice to forgiveness for personal sin. Paul's metaphor that Jesus was the first of the martyrs to be raised into God's justice, and that therefore the general bodily resurrection of all the martyrs had begun (which meant that God at last was acting to establish God's justice on earth) got reduced to the mundane and hopeless conviction that death

29

literally no longer happens to those who believe that Jesus forgives trespass.

Those who want to argue about the importance of personal sin can immerse themselves in Paul's letter to the Romans. For now, the point is that when we follow Jesus's teaching and love our enemies, and when we accept Jesus's invitation to participate in God's distributive justice, sin disappears. Salvation means liberation from injustice through participation in the Kingdom, NOT obeying specific individual moral rules.

It's easy to follow moral rules. Human history suggests the real struggle lies in opposing the normalcy of civilization's Empire. Empire is not only found in governments, although governments at all levels are prime examples. Empire is found increasingly in corporations that oppress workers with impunity. Everyone knows about the Wal-Marts and Enrons of the commercial world, but the petty tyrannies of law firms, church councils, university department chairs, management theories that leave no room for truly independent thinking, all contribute to the equalizing, socializing, normalizing of unjust systems. As our Planet continues in its apparent transformation to a warmer environment, justice takes on a broader meaning than simply interactions among humans. We are beginning to realize that human well-being depends on clean air, potable and free water, and diversity of species among all beings – plant, animal, molecular, even viral. Growing corn to feed our gluttony for cheap fuel becomes an issue of distributive justice because of its impact on the human food supply, and on the balance of life itself.

And what of the doctrinal "personal savior" born to each one of us in this season? If Jesus is my personal savior and lord, then in order to participate in God's Kingdom I need to vote for tax increases that will fund state medicare programs so that the state won't seize my mother's house to reimburse end-of-life nursing home expenses; I need to responsibly dispose of toxic household waste such as computer monitors and old paint, even if it means paying for special pick-ups; I must avoid shopping at Wal-Mart, even though it means driving farther and paying more for food, clothing, and other essential items.

I can remind everyone I meet that Matthew's story about the three sages who followed some astrological phenomenon to the doorway of a house where a special two-year old was living can point to a reversal of Christianity as imperial triumph. What is important is not the wealth and power represented by gold, frankincense and myrrh, but the results prayed for by the long-ago celebrant at the coronation of King Solomon: "Give the king your justice, O God, and your righteousness to a king's son. . . . May he judge your people with righteousness, and your poor with justice. . . . for he delivers the needy when they call . . . from oppression and violence he redeems their life; and precious is their blood in his sight. . . ."

Signs and Wonders
Second Sunday after Epiphany

1 Corinthians 12:1-11; John 2:1-11

At this point in the readings we have taken a sharp turn away from anything resembling history remembered, and are deep into the formative mythology of the early Christian way. Perhaps the reason for this diversion on the part of the creators of the RCL is that once Jesus had been baptized and had by God's declaration replaced John the Baptist in terms of importance, the next credential Jesus would need is some kind of sign of his miraculous prowess. First century folk were very familiar with magic and miracle. For Jesus to be reported as turning water into wine at a wedding was no more surprising than raising the dead. It was not metaphor; it was confirmation that he was indeed the longed-for Messiah.

Coupled with the story of the wedding at Cana is the portion of Paul's first letter to the community at Corinth in which he spells out the gifts of the "Spirit." The standard Christian sermon is easy to write: As Jesus turned water into wine, so believers in Jesus have gifts of the same "Spirit": wisdom, knowledge, faith, healing, prophecy, discernment of spirits, tongues, and the interpretation of tongues. "All these are activated by one and the same Spirit," writes Paul, "who allots to each one individually just as the Spirit chooses." The literal interpretation of all this has led to dozens of Christian denominations, hierarchies of church leadership, and other manifestations of the seemingly unavoidable complicity of the Church with the "normalcy of civilization," marching into Empire.

But if Christian exiles are to take these readings seriously, the question to ask is not "how could this possibly be true?" but "what can it mean?" In 1988, Martin Scorcese produced a film version of Nikkos Katzanzakis's novel, *The Last Temptation of Christ*. The film scandalized the Christian Right, was protested and boycotted, and made lots of money. At the end of the dramatization of the wedding at Cana, Jesus sits in the middle of a celebrating, dancing, singing, crowd, and as the camera pulls back, he raises his cup and winks. It is a surprising and provocative interpretation of the character of the savior of the world. Jesus is a party animal. But why not have fun in the Kingdom of God? Not only do the lilies of the field decline to toil and spin, look how they dance and play in the wind.

Paul's list of the free gifts of the Spirit also deserves reconsideration.

Paul is writing to a specific community about how to live in a community that has accepted Jesus's invitation to participate in the ongoing manifestation of the Kingdom of God on earth. Paul and the communities he founded believed that the general resurrection of all the martyrs for God's justice had begun with Jesus's death and resurrection, and that the establishment of God's Kingdom was imminent. The Corinthians were first century people. They knew about magic and miracle. They expected that they and their leaders would be healers, prophets, perhaps even mediums, able to speak in tongues, and to interpret the messages of those who speak in tongues. Paul is telling them that these gifts are from God to be used for the common good. In the community that follows Jesus's way, all these gifts are "activated by the same Spirit." So there is no hierarchy here. The same God, the same Spirit, the same Jesus speaks to each person in the community. Later, Paul will declare that all are one *in Christ*, no difference between male, female, slave, or free. The gifts are to be used in the ongoing work of establishing God's justice-compassion.

What are the signs and wonders of participation in God's Kingdom today? What are the gifts of the Spirit in the twenty-first century community of exiles from Christian tradition? There are mystical answers to these questions, but postmodern minds are leery.

Paul was a mystic, and expected the members of his communities to also be mystics. John Dominic Crossan goes so far as to suggest that Paul thought that only mystics could be Christians, and that all Christians must be mystics.[10] Suppose that in order to participate in God's Kingdom in the twenty-first century, we were to substitute the word "believer" for "mystic."

---

[10]Crossan and Reed, *In Search of Paul*, 280.

Traditional and conservative Christians today, who call themselves "progressive," are blasting the so-called "secular liberals" for denying the importance of religion, and for rejecting the reality of "Spirit." Somehow, these Christians have the idea that only believers in Jesus (mystics) can choose to participate in God's Kingdom.

What if the gifts of the Spirit in today's world are nonviolence, and the talents and qualities of mind that result in justice-compassion? Suppose that all acts of justice-compassion are evidence of participation in God's Kingdom? Paul wrote in his letter, "Now there are varieties of gifts, but the same Spirit; and there are varieties of services, but the same Lord; and there are varieties of activities, but it is the same God who activates all of them in everyone." If so-called "progressive" Christians are going to apply literally Paul's first century words meant for a specific group to the twenty-first century, then "everyone" means "everyone."

Kingdom Community Part One
Third Sunday after Epiphany

*Nehemiah 8:1-10; Psalm 19; 1 Corinthians 12:12-31a;
Luke 4:14-21*

The second, third, and fourth Sundays after the Epiphany follow Paul's First Letter to the Corinthians, and Luke's continuing saga of the life and teachings of Jesus. In the readings for the third Sunday, the Law of Moses is superseded by the authority of Jesus, and fulfilled in the mystical body of Christ – the members of the Church Triumphant. The creators of the RCL have really laid it all out for us. What a marvel! God's Plan for Humanity is so obvious, how could anyone miss the point?

Paul probably wrote the letter because rebellious members of the fledgling community in Corinth were on the verge of throwing in with Rome's imperial theology rather than God's justice-compassion. Roman society functioned in a system of patronage from the top down and from the inside out. Jesus's open table and Paul's declaration that in the Christian community all are equal and all spiritual gifts are to be used for the good of all in the community caused problems for people used to hierarchical seating arrangements at banquets, and using their talents to further improve their own social and economic standing. To make matters worse, Paul taught that in the Christian community (the body of Christ) no member was more important than another, and that the one who gave up all thought of reward or personal gain in the service of the community was more valuable than the one to whom the most social or economic debt was owed.

These readings from Paul's letter to the Corinthians are so familiar as to have nearly lost any real meaning, perhaps because the Church has become so aligned with imperial theology that we can't see the revolution in Paul's teaching that the powerlessness illustrated in Jesus's crucifixion – a criminal's death – is the ultimate illustration of the omnipotence of God. Paul writes, "God has so arranged the human body, giving the greater honor to the inferior member, that there can be no dissension within the body. . . . If one member suffers, all suffer together with it; if one member is honored, all rejoice together with it." Paul is not talking about "teamwork" or "cooperation" among members of a community. He is talking about *kenosis*.

Traditional theology has used the term "kenosis" (emptying out) to describe one side of a debate over whether the divine nature of Jesus was renounced at the time of his appearance in human form. This argument serves as a convenient way to divert attention from the fact that the institutional Church has, almost from the beginning, aligned Christian tradition and belief with the prevailing political power – in Crossan's words, with the "normalcy of civilization." So long as the Church is engaged in a debate about the balance of divinity versus humanity in Jesus Christ, so long as the people are distracted by the superstition that Jesus's death means a literal ticket to heaven – with maybe a stop in purgatory along the way (after all, grace can't really mean what Paul says it means), then emperors, kings, entrepreneurs, capitalists, governors, parents, academicians, bosses of every stripe can claim power over everyone and anyone and can manipulate injustice to their own benefit with impunity. The normalcy of civilization chugs on relegating the Kingdom of God to pie-in-the-sky.

Crossan suggests that rather than being a mysterious supernatural act whereby God gave up God's divinity in order to become human, *kenosis* means a god/spirit that does not intervene, does not threaten, but offers life and abundance to all without questioning the value of the individual life form; and microcosmically, a person or a community that does not act in its own economic, political, or military self-interest, but insists on fairness. This is the foolishness of life in Christ. This is how life is to be lived in God's Kingdom, now, on earth, in the ongoing struggle for justice-compassion in opposition to social convention, economic and political rules, retributive reward and punishment, i.e., the ways of the world, the sins of the flesh – Empire.

Kingdom Community Part Two
Fourth Sunday after Epiphany

Jeremiah 1:4-10; 1 Corinthians 13:1-13; Psalm 71:1-6;
Luke 4:21-30

Traditionally, the Christian Church has viewed the Old Testament of the Bible as the prelude to the New Covenant with God secured by Jesus's death and resurrection. The prophets are calling the people to repentance, and to return to God so that ultimately everyone, dead and alive, will be saved and reconciled to God through Jesus Christ. So this week, the prophet Jeremiah is called and commissioned by God, who tells Jeremiah, "Before I formed you in the womb I knew you, and before you were born I consecrated you; I appointed you a prophet to the nations." Echos of the prologue to John's Gospel: "In the beginning was the Word and the Word was with God, and the Word was God"; and Luke puts into the mouth of the newly-baptized and ordained Jesus, "Today this scripture has been fulfilled in your hearing."

Jesus was referring to the passage from Isaiah that was quoted in the previous commentary, but the point is taken. God knew Jesus as well as or better than he knew Jeremiah. Unlike Jeremiah, however, who protests that he's only a boy and can't possibly accept this awesome appointment, Jesus simply hands the rolled up scroll back to the attendant. The law is no longer necessary. The doctrine of predestination of the elect of God starts here. After Jesus's astounding claim, his sermon on how prophets are not accepted in their hometown bombs, and as predicted, his friends and neighbors throw him out of town. But he is a magic spirit, as well as a man, and he "passed through the midst of them and went on his way." Poof! Merlin could not have done it with greater aplomb.

Likewise, the sermon from Paul to the "church" in Corinth continues the fulfillment of God's intervention on earth, as the people learn the rules of love. How many marriages have been sealed with the words "Love is patient; love is kind; love is not envious or boastful or arrogant or rude. It does not insist on its own way; it is not irritable or resentful . . . [love] bears all things, believes all things, hopes all things, endures all things . . . And now faith, hope, and love abide, these three; and the greatest of these is love"? Pass the Kleenex. The King James version doesn't use the word love, but the word "charity." So now the greatest of the three is tax-deductible contributions to your favorite social program – the one that devotes the greatest percentage of its income to hands-on work.

Is this really what these scriptures are pointing to?

John Dominic Crossan speaks of a *kenotic god* who does not need to intervene, whose presence is life and justice-compassion, and whose absence is injustice and death. Somehow a postmodern mind like Crossan's can let go of the need for the kind of reality that can be literally touched, tasted, seen, heard, smelled, and can experience a numinous, inclusive mysticism. We cannot know if it is the same mystic reality that premodern minds like Paul or the writers of Jeremiah or Psalm 71 may have experienced – certainly postmodern minds make vastly different assumptions about the nature of the cosmos – but the experience of the seamlessness of human life with the known universe must be analogous. We can't ask Jeremiah, but we can resonate with the truth of the words he channeled: "Before I formed you in the womb I knew you, and before you were born I consecrated you" – made you holy. To what end? To be. To participate in God's justice-compassion. The psalmist sings praises for God, "for you are my rock and my fortress. . . . I have been like a portent to many, but you are my strong refuge." God is not an intervener, but a matrix of power formed in the original flaming forth of the cosmos. Does that mean that nothing bad ever happens? Of course not. It means that our lives are intimately bound up in the universal web of space-time, and grounded in the balance of energies that constitute life on earth. It means I have faith in the inherent goodness of that ongoing, unfinished, ever-evolving tapestry, which is God's Kingdom.

Paul could not imagine an incomplete pattern. He and those who understood what he was trying to say thought that while the establishment of God's Kingdom was a work in progress, begun with the resurrection of Jesus, the completion would come in their lifetime. Not the end of time, but the completion of the struggle for justice-compassion. Paul's letter to the community in Corinth, struggling with the powers and principalities of social norms and conventions, says over and over again that community in Christ means the kind of radical sharing and equality that God's Kingdom illustrates. Belief in Jesus's story is not the defining factor. Love – compassion – is. "Love never ends," writes Paul, "but as for prophecies . . . tongues . . . knowledge . . . when the complete comes, the partial will come to an end. . . . Now I know only in part; then I will know fully, even as I have been fully known." To participate in that kind of community in the twenty-first century is to participate in the seamless realm of an ever-changing cosmos – a conscious incarnation of the realm of God.

Food for Thought
February 2 – The Presentation of the Lord[11]

*Malachi 3:1-4; Psalm 84 or Psalm 24:7-10; Hebrews 2:14-18;
Luke 2:22-40*

In the midst of the liturgical progression from Epiphany to
Lent, tradition calls the church back to the mundane details of
Jesus's infancy. Luke's Chapter 2 fills in the story from birth to
circumcision to presentation as the first-born son to the coming-
of-age of a gifted religious leader anointed by God. In *The First
Christmas*[12] Borg and Crossan suggest that Luke's purpose was
to set up the birth of the Jewish Messiah as a counter to the
birth of the Roman Caesar – also hailed as "Savior, Redeemer,
Son of God." The scene in the temple in Jerusalem confirms the
child Jesus as the expected one who would redeem Israel from
bondage to imperial injustice and oppression.

Luke's story is grounded in the mandate in Leviticus 12,
which requires the mother to follow specific rites of purification
forty days after giving birth. But the creators of the RCL seem
to overturn Luke's references to Leviticus 12 by bringing in
verses out of context from the prophet Malachi. The result is
that Malachi's messenger is assumed by supercessionary
Christian tradition to be John the Baptist, who is sent from God
to announce the sudden coming of the Lord to his temple. That
Lord (Jesus) "will purify the descendents of Levi. . . . Then the
offering of Judah and Jerusalem will be pleasing to the Lord."
Why? Here a subtle, unquestioned, anti-Semitism seeps
through. The offerings of Judah and Jerusalem are now pleasing
to God because the people have been purified of the old, Jewish
religion.

In Malachi's own context, the sons of Levi have been
purified by the Lord through a process that burns away
faithlessness to God's covenant. God's covenant is not about

---

[11]This essay replaces the readings for the Fifth Sunday
after the Epiphany: *Isaiah 6:1-13; Psalm 138; 1 Cor. 15:1-
11; Luke 5:1-11.*

[12]Borg and Crossan, *The First Christmas*.

belief. God's covenant is about active, distributive, justice-compassion. If the liturgist does not stop at Malachi 3:4, but reads on to verse 5, God's judgment is made clear: "I will be swift to bear witness against the sorcerers, against the adulterers, against those who swear falsely, against those who oppress the hired workers in their wages, the widow and the orphan, against those who thrust aside the alien, and do not fear me, says the Lord of hosts."

The tradition of the Presentation of the Lord dates from the fourth century, and by the time the RCL was put together, the emphasis of Malachi on the coming of the Lord's justice was overtaken by the theology of the writer of the letter to the Hebrews. The language has deviated from salvation as liberation from injustice to salvation as freedom from the fear of death and the "one who has the power of death, that is, the devil. . . ."

The writer of Hebrews, a sermon written about the same time as Luke was writing his gospel and his sequel, the Book of Acts, pulls together much of the Hebrew scriptures and uses them to develop a particular Christology, which has little if anything to do with God's covenant of distributive justice-compassion, or with Luke's subversive suggestion that Jesus the Christ came to establish God's rule in opposition to the empire of Rome. Instead, again, verses are taken out of context to emphasize tradition. The writer is in the midst of setting up an argument that Jesus became the mediator between people and God – the High Priest. In order to achieve that position, Jesus had to first experience "the suffering of death, so that by the grace of God he might taste death for everyone" (Heb. 2:9). Because of that suffering, he was purified, and achieved the position as High Priest so that he could "make a sacrifice of atonement for the sins of the people" with his own body and blood. The ultimate sin, according to this writer, is unbelief in Jesus as the High Priest of God – the refusal of the people to accept the "better covenant, enacted through better promises" (Heb. 8:6-7) – more subtle anti-Semitism.

The festival of the Presentation of the Lord may have begun as a celebration of the revelation of light, even rebirth from the darkness of political oppression to liberation and

41

covenant with God's realm of distributive justice-compassion, but the Hebrews passage casts the pall of substitutionary atonement over the festivities. Given the vagaries of the Christian liturgical calendar, which has to deal with the moon-based movable feast called Easter, the verses from Hebrews 2:14-18 perhaps serve to remind the people of the coming season of Lent.

The organizers of Christian tradition were masters of the appropriation of local cultural myth and metaphor. The Christ was nearly immediately defined as "the light of the world" (John 1:1-6). Luke's Simeon sings what became known in Catholic liturgy as the *nunc dimitis*: "Now let your servant depart in peace according to your word, for my eyes have seen your salvation, which you have prepared in the presence of all peoples, a light for revelation to all Gentiles and for glory to your people Israel." The date for the presentation has varied, depending on when Jesus's birth was supposed to have occurred. Once December 25 was agreed upon (as opposed to January 6), February 2 became the day. February 2 is the time in the Planet's yearly orbit around the sun, halfway between solstice and equinox (15 degrees Aquarius), when, in the northern hemisphere, the light noticeably changes from the darkness of winter to the increasing brightness of spring.

In northern agricultural life, this time of year brings the first births of livestock, and milk and eggs once again become available, if not plentiful. The Celtic Goddess of Wisdom, Bride ("breed"), in charge of poetry, smithcraft, and healing, became the Christian saint Brigid, who was reputed to have been the wet nurse for the baby Jesus. Brigid's feast day is February 1, which conveniently appropriates the old pre-Christian festival celebrating rebirth and the increasing light (Imbolc). Milk and milk products (cheeses, butter) are on the menu for the feast. The festival mass for this day is called Candlemas. As the light returns to the world, the Christ is revealed.

This festival can be reclaimed, using the metaphors of justice-compassion from Malachi, Psalm 24, and Luke. The prophet Malachi challenges the leaders of the people to take care of the oppressed; the writer of the psalm says that those who are authorized to "ascend the hill of the Lord" and come into the temple are those "with clean hands and pure hearts, who do not lift up their souls to what is false." Old Simeon says he can die in peace, now that he has seen the one who will be a light to all the world. Anna speaks "about the child to all who were waiting for the liberation of Jerusalem."

The festival can be reclaimed using the metaphors of the natural world, the ultimate wisdom of the created universe, in which no being is denied the abundance assured by God's covenant of distributive justice-compassion, with a Eucharist of milk and honey, bread and wine.

One: Ho! Everyone who thirsts, come to the waters; and those who have no money, come, buy and eat! Come, buy wine and milk without price, for our God calls us away from oppression and greed to a realm of justice and love [pour wine].
God calls us away from famine and poverty to an abundance of milk and honey [pour milk].
Wisdom orders all things well: First the grain, then the ear, then the full grain in the ear [break bread].
To inherit Wisdom is as sweet as the honeycomb [pour honey into a bowl].
Wisdom has set her table. She calls from the highest places, "Come, eat of my bread and drink of the wine I have mixed. Come, for all has been made ready."
[All are invited to come to the table, dip bread into milk, honey or wine. Take as many pieces of bread as is desired. Some may wish to feed one another.]

Paul's Resurrection Theology Part One:
If Christ Has Not Been Raised
Sixth Sunday after Epiphany

*1 Corinthians 15:1-20; Luke 6:17-26; Jeremiah 17:5-10;
Psalm 1*

John Dominic Crossan, in his collaborative work with Jonathan L. Reed,[13] proposes that Paul – a Pharisee – saw the resurrection of Jesus as the first indication that the general resurrection of the martyrs to God's justice had begun. Crossan points out that people rising from the grave was not an unusual occurrence in first century Greek and Roman cultures. Further, the people Paul was corresponding with in Rome were familiar with Platonic concepts of the immortality of the soul, and would have interpreted Paul's "resurrection of the body" in that way. So in his first letter to the community in Corinth, Paul presents his argument about why Jesus's resurrection is NOT the immortality of the soul, but the beginning of God's action in the world to restore God's justice-compassion, God's Kingdom, in direct contradiction and opposition to the divinity of Caesar and the injustice of Caesar's Empire.

The reading from 1 Corinthians 15 for the sixth Sunday after the Epiphany is verses 12-20. However, it is important to include verses 1-11 (from the fifth Sunday lectionary) as prologue.

Crossan argues that the writer of Luke/Acts essentially had no time for Paul as an apostle. Luke and the Jewish Christians in Jerusalem maintained that only the original twelve called by Jesus could be considered authentic apostles. Paul was considered to be a missionary to the gentiles in the Roman world outside of Jerusalem. So Paul is answering that criticism in verses 1-11 by claiming legitimacy as an apostle because, like them, Jesus "appeared to Cephas, then to the twelve, then he appeared to more than five hundred brothers and sisters at one time . . . then he appeared to James, then to all the apostles.

---

[13]Crossan and Reed, *In Search of Paul*.

Last of all, as to one untimely born, he appeared also to me." Even though Paul considered himself "unfit to be called an apostle because I persecuted the church of God," through the grace (free gift) of God, he was called to the work.

Then Paul proceeds with his argument (verses 12-20) – which seems circular to most Christians hearing these passages again for maybe the sixth or the twentieth time, depending on the number of years spent in Sunday School, or listening to various preachers or lay leaders read these passages whenever Year C rolls around. Believers' eyes will generally glaze over as Paul obfuscates: "If there is no resurrection of the dead, then Christ has not been raised; and if Christ has not been raised, then our proclamation . . . and your faith [have] been in vain. We are even found to be misrepresenting God because we testified of God that he raised Christ – whom he did not raise if it is true that the dead are not raised. . . ." The traditionalists know that Jesus rose from the dead, so why bother with this argument? And postmodern exiles from tradition know that Jesus never walked in resuscitated body out of the tomb – stories of Elvis Presley notwithstanding, nobody comes back from the dead in the twenty-first century. It's much easier for both traditionalists and exiles to stick with the story Luke writes (the "sermon on the plain") and rail against sinful people who persecuted the prophets, killed Jesus, and continue to oppress the poor. But if Crossan's interpretation of Paul is correct, and the 2,000 years of Platonic gloss and church dogma can be put aside, Paul's argument to the first century Corinthians becomes a passionate call to participate in God's Kingdom here and now.

Paul was a Pharisee who believed that, at some time, God would act to bring God's justice to earth. When that happened, it would only be fair that the people who had died before God's justice was restored would be allowed to take part. Otherwise, people who had given their lives in the service of God's law and righteousness would have died in vain. So the idea developed that when God's justice was restored, there would be a general resurrection of the dead so that they could also participate in God's Kingdom. When Paul first heard the story about Jesus's resurrection from the dead, he considered it blasphemy. After his mystical experience on the road to

45

Damascus, he realized that God's great intervention to restore God's righteous Kingdom on earth had begun. The signal for the general resurrection of those who had died in the service of God's justice was the resurrection of Jesus. In Paul's metaphor, Jesus, the Christ, the one chosen by God for this task, "has been raised from the dead, the first fruits of those who have died."

The key to understanding what this means lies in the verb tense used in Paul's argument. "Christ *has been* raised." Paul expected that the task of restoring God's Kingdom would be completed within his lifetime, but the point is that the task had begun, and was an ongoing process. At the end of Chapter 15, he writes, "Therefore, my beloved, be steadfast, immovable, always excelling in the work of the Lord [justice-compassion], because you know that in the Lord [in partnership with the risen Christ] your labor is not in vain."

In today's world of reactionary literalism, the Christ metaphor is nearly impossible to reclaim. Liberal mystics are just as reluctant as secular mystics to indulge in Jesus- and God-talk. But if Christianity is going to have any meaning in a postmodern secular society, exiles must speak up and claim Christ crucified and transformed; God's Kingdom comes here and now in the choices we make for nonviolence, justice-compassion, and peace.

Paul's Resurrection Theology Part Two: Death Has Been Swallowed Up in Victory Seventh Sunday after Epiphany (Transfiguration Sunday)

Exodus 34:29-35; 1 Corinthians 15:35-58;
2 Corinthians 3:12-4:2; Luke 9:28-36

The RCL provides for ten Sundays between Epiphany and Ash Wednesday. The last Sunday before Ash Wednesday is designated "Transfiguration Sunday." Luke continues his proof that Jesus is more than the old Moses, the original law-giver, more than the old Elijah, the first to be bodily taken up into heaven. In the Exodus passage, Moses's face shines with the light of God so that he has to wear a veil when he delivers the law to the people. Jesus's whole body, including his clothing, shines with a great white light, and the awed disciples share a vision of Moses and Elijah, the two most important prophets in Jewish tradition, talking with Jesus about what he is planning to accomplish in Jerusalem.

Perhaps for the sake of dogma, the readings for Epiphany into Lent leave out Paul's discourse on how the dead are raised and what is the nature of the transformed body (unless there are a minimum of eight Sundays before Ash Wednesday). Instead we are treated to a veiled insult to the Jerusalem establishment, who "to this very day, whenever Moses [the law] is read, a veil lies over their minds; but when one turns to the Lord the veil is removed" (2 Corinthians 3:15-16).

In Paul's view, the general resurrection had begun with Jesus's resurrection. The transformation of human life on earth from the laws of Empire to the distributive justice-compassion of God's Kingdom had begun, and the process would be complete within Paul's lifetime. So in 1 Corinthians 15:50, he sets up his discussion of what the spiritual body might be like when the process is complete. "What I am saying . . . is this: flesh and blood cannot inherit the Kingdom of God . . .[but] Listen, I will tell you a mystery! We will not all die, but we will all be changed, in a moment, in the twinkling of an eye . . . ."

Can Paul's argument stand in a postmodern world? ". . . [N]o Jesus resurrection, no general resurrection; no general resurrection, no Jesus resurrection"[14]: only in the sense that if Jesus had not died in defiance of the Roman Empire, and if Paul had not interpreted that death as a counter to the divinity of Caesar, who would stand against the normalcy of civilization? Just as Jesus said, the Kingdom of God is here, now, within you, if you will only open your eyes and ears and look and listen. The trumpet sounds, and we realize that we can choose to live and participate in that Kingdom, which has nothing to do with Caesar's Empire, and everything to do with nonviolent distributive justice.

So what? What is nonviolence? What is distributive justice-compassion? The more useful question may be what is violence, and what is Empire? Violence is anything that results in the invalidation of life. Empire is what keeps that invalidation in place. Whenever a child is prevented from asking questions or pursuing her natural talent because of governmental or social rules about what is necessary to be mastered in a classroom, Empire prevails. Whenever another life form – whether an intimate family member or a portion of an ecosystem – is used or abused for a purpose other than its own, it is subjected to violence. All human systems are prone to violent Empire. That is the struggle. That is what is meant in Paul's second letter to the Corinthians – who apparently did not get it the first time around – when Paul says, "We have renounced the shameful things that one hides; we refuse to practice cunning or to falsify God's word . . . And even if our gospel is veiled [it is because] the god of this world has blinded the minds of the unbelievers to keep them from seeing the light of the gospel of the glory of Christ, who is the image of God."

Who is the god of this world? Not so-called "Satan," and certainly and unequivocally not "the Jews" – which is inferred by orthodox tradition – but commercial and social normalcy: Meister Eckhart's "merchant mentality,"[15] which cannot participate in the Kingdom because justice-compassion is bad

---

[14]Ibid., 342.

[15]Fox, *Breakthrough*, 450.

for business and a detriment to political power. To sin is to not participate in God's justice-compassion, and therefore to be dead to God's Kingdom, and it is not physical death, but the law of Empire that cuts us off from justice-compassion. "The sting of death is sin," writes Paul, "and the power of sin is the law. But thanks be to God who gives us the victory through our Lord Jesus Christ."

Lent

Ash Wednesday: Change the Paradigm

Joel 2:1-2; 12-17; Matthew 6:1-6, 16-21

Generally, Ash Wednesday and Lent make little sense in today's world. The season is spring, and winter is in retreat. The whole Earth will shortly burst into life; why focus on death? Jesus probably did not recommend fasting for his followers. The entire section of Matthew 6, recommended reading for this day, is in black print in the Jesus Seminar's *Five Gospels*, indicating that Jesus very probably said none of it.

Christians – at least in the West – visit the local church or cathedral for a spot of ashes on the forehead, then return to lives that have little to do with forty days of fasting and prayer. Depriving oneself of chocolate or meat might work for a while. Going off booze and cigarettes could be a good thing if one does not return to the old ways at the end of Holy Week. But Ash Wednesday is on the calendar, and it can take on metaphor, and call for serious reflection. As the prophet Joel preaches, some reckoning from God is coming, so be warned.

"Rend your hearts and not your clothing," God says. Rebuild cities ravaged by natural disasters. End the holocausts of war, famine, disease, and death. "Blow the trumpet in Zion," the prophet writes, "sanctify a fast: call a solemn assembly; gather the people; sanctify the congregation . . . . Let them say, 'Spare your people, O Lord, and do not make your heritage a mockery, a byword among the nations.' Why should it be said among the peoples, 'Where is their God'?"

Where indeed is the God of the people of these United States? In Walmart? At the bank? In the Congressional Budget Office? The better question might be "Who is their God?" Neglect, Retribution, Betrayal, Violence, and Greed? Or Justice, Forgiveness, Love, Non-violence and Generosity?

Dr. Arthur J. Dewey of Xavier University has suggested a way to win the peace in the Middle East."Keep the trucks rolling," he said, trucks from Walmart, Home Depot, food and medical suppliers, rolling non-stop across the borders between Iraq and Iran, Syria, Jordan, and Saudi Arabia, accompanied by engineers, doctors, teachers, and organizers. A few would be lost, Dr. Dewey said, but not nearly as many as have been killed in the conflicts of the past few years. It is a model used on a small scale by Mahatma Ghandi in South Africa in the 1920s, and by Witness for Peace in Central America during the Reagan Contra wars and elsewhere. All that is required is people willing to provide accompaniment and hands-on rebuilding of a devastated society.

This is a different paradigm from the one most of the Planet lives in today. There is no room in this paradigm for military violence, the politics of acquisition, or the power struggles of religious systems. It is a shift from piety, war, victory to covenant, nonviolence, justice-compassion.

What better work for the season of Lent?

Power Corrupts – Or it Doesn't
Change the Paradigm II
First Sunday in Lent

Deuteronomy 26:1-11; Psalm 91:1-2, 9-16; Romans 10:8b-13;
Luke 4:1-13

Let's dispense with orthodoxy immediately: Lent is not about repenting for sins, whether great or small. Giving up chocolate or movies or being nice to your mother-in-law won't cut it. It is not about replicating the story of the people of Israel wandering in the desert for forty years because they had forgotten who brought them out of bondage; nor is Lent about replicating the experience of Jesus's possible sojourn among the Essenes in the wilderness, *if* that experience is interpreted to be reconciling himself to the fate God had already established for him.

In Luke's story, Jesus tells the devil not to put the Lord your God to the test, and then the text says that "when the devil had finished every test he departed from him until an opportune time." The master story-teller is foreshadowing the hero's final battle to the death when the devil (the evil spirit?) goes after Judas (22:3-6), and causes massive betrayal and abandonment by Jesus's disciples. Significantly, for orthodoxy, Jesus points away from himself in this initial skirmish, and neither the devil nor Luke apparently thinks that Jesus is God.

If John Dominic Crossan is onto something with his interpretation of Paul's mission to the Pagan/Gentile worlds outside Jerusalem,[16] it is only fair to start the reading from Romans 10 a little sooner than the cobblers who decided to start half-way through verse 8: "(that is, the word of faith that we proclaim)." The rest of the paragraph has been read to reinforce the dogma that if you believe that Jesus died for your sins, you will be saved (from hell and damnation). Who you are doesn't matter; *if* you believe that, you will be saved. But what is Paul's purpose? He is arguing that "Christ is the end of the law . . . ."

---

[16]Crossan and Reed, *In Search of Paul.*

55

The law has no power over the Christ. The law is meaningless. Whose law? The law of Empire. The law of Caesar. Because justice-compassion (righteousness) trumps the law of Empire by restoring God's covenant of distributive, nonviolent, justice-compassion. Whoever calls on this Lord – no distinction between Jew and Greek – anyone who claims God's nonviolent covenant of justice-compassion – is part of the great general raising into God's Kingdom. Whoever calls on this Lord is already transformed into the spiritual body of Christ, and does not need to fear the death that comes from selling out to the Empire. Whoever calls on this Lord is saved to integrity.

Well, I'm not selling out to the Empire, right? I don't shop at Walmart. I buy organic. I don't use credit cards. The chocolate is "fair trade" chocolate. I tell everyone the best way to "support the troops" is to bring them home ASAP.

Again, the meaning is far deeper than that.

Dr. Dewey suggests the story in Luke is an illustration of power: " . . . [T]his is a contest to decide which power is to rule the world. Is it to be the power that comes from magic? from manipulating things and people? from the desire to see oneself as great and in control? Or is it to be a power that refuses to display itself at the price of its own integrity?"[17]

One of the lies told by Empire is the definition of power as political, economic, social, and military/legal "power-over" the universe the Empire controls. Everyone who agrees with this definition is trapped in the systems that perpetuate poverty, war, and oppression because even in a democratic society, people will vote against their own welfare.[18] But in Luke's story, Jesus illustrates that to reject that kind of power (power-over) means to actualize his own. Jesus's power is power-with the justice-compassion of the Kingdom of God. To the extent that our own personal power is that kind of power, we effectively counter the seemingly inevitable progress of the normalcy of civilization into the strength of sin in the law of Empire.

---

[17]Dewey, *The Word in Time*, 156.

[18]For example, in 2006, evangelical Christian churches in the State of Alabama convinced their impoverished members to vote against raising taxes on the rich and eliminating or lowering taxes on themselves.

We are taught to reject personal power because we can't believe we can safely avoid the temptations the devil offers: manipulating things and people, and seeing ourselves as greater than others and most important of all, in control. Jesus refused to play those games because he realized that to play them meant losing himself: losing his integrity, losing his freedom to be himself. That is the great contradiction in the story of Jesus's death. It was not a hero's death. It was meant to be humiliating, reducing him and his power to nothing. There are some who would say that it did. If Jesus had allowed his personal power to be corrupted, they would be right.

One of the major ways we buy into the Empire's paradigm is to agree to ever-more-invasive incursions into our personal lives, from airport security searches to red-light cameras to drug-free employment and school activities policies that require everyone to submit to screenings whether there is probable cause or not. The mantra in this post-September 11 society is, "I've got nothing to hide." The second verse of the mantra is "It doesn't affect me." Injustice affects everyone, because the assumption is that everyone is guilty. As Paul writes in 1 Corinthians 15:56, "the sting of death is sin, and the power of sin is the law." The way to defeat that power is to believe in and act from our own integrity.

Sacrifice: To Make Sacred
Change the Paradigm III
Second Sunday in Lent

Genesis 15:1-12, 17-18; Psalm 27; Philippians 3:17-4:1;
Luke 13:31-35 (Luke 9:28-36)

Luke's vignette describing Jesus's lament over Jerusalem, claiming to follow the pre-ordained path to Calvary, is so familiar it no longer has any meaning. Even knowing that Luke was writing for one faction of Christians well after Jesus's death fails to inspire fresh interpretation. In a time when the line separating church and state is increasingly blurred by government funding of "faith based" social programs, and conservative religious social mores are written into the law of the land, it is difficult to imagine how to get outside the retributive, imperial paradigm. Jesus certainly seems to intend to speak to imperial power in Luke's story: "Go and tell that fox for me, 'Listen, I am casting out demons and performing cures today and tomorrow, and on the third day I finish my work.'" In contemporary language: "So screw you, Herod Antipas. Like, I'm leaving anyway because no prophet can be killed outside of Jerusalem." Petulant, at best, antisemitic at worst, Luke's Jesus slouches on his way to Golgotha to die.

The Genesis passages tell the story of God's covenant with Abram. A covenant is an agreement or contract drawn up under seal. In Judeo-Christian myth, the original covenant between God and humanity was sealed when God set his rainbow in the sky after the great flood. Now, God makes a second covenant with Abram. The creators of the RCL cut the story off before this second covenant is sealed, and it is too bad, because the imagery of how the covenant is sealed lends palpable wonder and mystery to the later interpretations of the story of Jesus. Abram wants to know how he will know that he will indeed possess the land that God has promised. God tells him to prepare "a heifer three years old, a female goat three years old, a ram three years old, a turtledove, and a young pigeon" for sacrifice. Abram does all this, and then spends time chasing away the birds of prey who of course see an opportunity for a feast. Eventually, "As the sun was going down, a deep sleep fell upon Abram, and a deep and terrifying darkness descended upon him," and God speaks to him out of the darkness. This part is left out of the reading. God spells out specifically what will happen within four hundred years (four generations). The people will be aliens in a land not theirs, but God will deliver them. Abram himself will die in peace, and then the people will return to the land in the fourth generation. The covenant is sealed when "a smoking fire pot and a flaming torch passed between these pieces" of the sacrifice, assuring Abram that he can trust God's promises.

The metaphor of sacrifice to seal a covenant is basic to Luke's story about the life and teaching of Jesus (see Luke 2:21-24). In Luke 13:31-35, Jesus declares that contrary to the covenant with Abram, which would take four generations to implement, the covenant with Jesus will take three days. Because we know the stories, we know that Jesus's life will be the sacrifice that seals the new covenant. Paul also uses the metaphor of sacrifice, but unlike Luke, it is in direct contradiction to the Roman civic religion, wherein citizens made sacrifices to the living deified Caesar and feasted with their clients, and it is that metaphor that is behind his words to the group in Philippi: "For many live as the enemies of the cross of Christ . . . . Their end is destruction; their god is the belly; and their glory is in their shame; their minds are set on earthly things." But then Paul gets political. "But our *citizenship*" he says "is in heaven, and it is from there that . . . Christ will transform the body of our humiliation . . ." – just as God acted in Abram's dream to pass the torch across the prepared sacrifice – "that it may be conformed to the body of his glory by the power that also enables him to make all things *subject to himself*" – another political, anti-imperial statement. Paul continues to insist on "citizenship" for Christians "in heaven," NOT citizenship in Rome. "Citizenship" is a political term, used deliberately to remind the hearers of Paul's letter that their loyalty is to the risen Christ, not to the pantheon of Caesar. Luke, by contrast, lays the responsibility for the death of Jesus at God's door, not Caesar's – where it truly belongs. In fact, the victim – Jesus – actively chooses to play the role God has ordained for him. The Romans are off the hook in Luke's gospel. Luke's religion is no threat to Roman imperial injustice. Paul's theology, however, written fifty to seventy-five years earlier, undermines the whole system.

So what is the imperial paradigm in the twenty-first century that we are called to transform, and conform to the body of Christ's glory? Or, in other words, how do we participate in the Kingdom of God's justice-compassion – which is what is meant by "the body of Christ's glory"? We who are followers of Jesus's way are the body of Christ, and living in God's Kingdom means being conformed to that, in Paul's mystical, problematic, first century language.

In contrast to the imperial theology of piety, war, victory, and peace, John D. Crossan suggests Covenant, nonviolence, justice-compassion. But with whom is the Covenant, and how is it sealed? How do we sanctify opposition to imperial piety (such as service to war as "sacrifice") in a context of justice-compassion when in a secular society there is no "God"? Perhaps part of the answer is found in what we know about the nature of the universe. In *The Universe Story*,[19] Brian Swimme and Thomas Berry find the metaphor of Willing Sacrifice in the ongoing evolution of life forms that come into being, and if they find a niche, live and thrive, and if they do not, give way to life forms that can. ". . . [T]he universe has what can be called a sacrificial dimension. When we reflect upon the omnipresence of destruction and violence throughout the layered universe, and on the mysterious relationship of this destruction to the evocation of a great beauty, we can begin to approach such an understanding. . . . [T]he human community is attempting to give recognition to a central dimension of existence and to enter this reality in a creative rather than an unconscious and destructive manner."

With that in mind, perhaps we can read Psalm 27 as confirmation of Covenant with distributive justice-compassion: "Teach me your way O Lord, and lead me on a level path because of my enemies. Do not give me up to the will of my

---

[19]Swimme and Berry, *The Universe Story* 59-60.

adversaries, for false witnesses have risen against me, and they are breathing out violence. I believe that I shall see the goodness of the Lord in the land of the living."

Collusion and Consequences
Change the Paradigm IV:
Third Sunday in Lent

Isaiah 55:1-9; Psalm 63:1-8; 1 Corinthians 10:1-13;
Luke 13:1-9

The readings for this third Sunday in Lent illustrate the eternal human spiritual tension between a violent and a nonviolent God: God's justice as distributive compassion versus God's justice as divine retribution.

Isaiah 55 is a hymn to pastoral, nonviolent, justice-compassion as the final Great Feast, when God at last establishes God's Kingdom: ". . . so shall my word be that goes out from my mouth: it shall not return to me empty, but it shall accomplish that which I purpose, and succeed in the thing for which I sent it." Why not go on and finish the hymn: "For you shall go out in joy, and be led back in peace . . . instead of the briar shall come up the myrtle; and it shall be to the Lord for a memorial, for an everlasting sign that shall not be cut off."

By contrast, Luke's Jesus is clearly the son of a violent god: "[U]nless you repent, you will all perish . . .," he says – twice. Apparently Jesus's God is inclined to give Luke's hearers one more chance before cutting them down, but that hardly translates into compassion.

The usual interpretation of the cherry-picked portion of Paul's first letter to the Corinthians is also a warning of the consequences of "desiring" evil. "God was not pleased with most of [the Israelites], and they were struck down in the wilderness. . . . So if you think you are standing, watch out that you do not fall." The litany of sins is fairly short, but comprehensive: idolatry, sexual immorality, trying God's (Christ's) patience, and complaining. In the traditional reading, Paul does have faith that whatever the test is that God sends, he will "provide the way out so that you may be able to endure it." Hope for salvation is the orthodox emphasis, not distributive justice and grace.

The cobblers of today's readings want us to think of "living water," from Isaiah's invitation to "Come to the waters," to the magic well (Numbers 21:17), which Paul – possibly echoed in John's gospel – calls Christ. But Paul's use of the story reinforces the imminent establishment of God's Kingdom of justice-compassion rather than retribution for non-belief in Jesus.

In his quick review of the story of God's delivery of the Israelites, Paul says, "all passed through the sea, and all were baptized into Moses in the cloud and in the sea, and all ate the same spiritual food, and all drank the same spiritual drink. For they drank from the spiritual rock that followed them, and the rock was Christ." These are metaphors derived from Jesus's teachings and the very earliest ideas of the emerging Jewish Christian community. The fact that Paul refers to that rock as "Christ" seems at first glance to reflect the theology found in the Gospel of John, or refer to the metaphor Matthew's Jesus uses to describe Peter, upon which "rock I will build my church" (Matthew 16:18). But Paul is writing to the Corinthians 50 to 100 years before Matthew and John's gospels were written and circulated. The spiritual rock that followed the Israelites in their journey through the wilderness seems instead to refer to a legend about the Israelites' sojourn in the desert, in which a rock-shaped, movable well followed them, providing water, grass for their flocks, and healing herbs. "About the size of an oven or beehive, it rolled along after the wanderers through hills and valleys and, when they camped, . . . gave everyone a drink at the door of his tent."[20] Even though the people sinned against God, God gave them this magic rock, which saved them and allowed them to reach the promised land. In the same way, Christ saves those who participate in God's justice-compassion, allowing them to live in God's Kingdom – coming within Paul's lifetime, and evidenced by the death and resurrection of Jesus.

"The power of the sword" of Psalm 63 is the evil that Paul is preaching against: the idolatry of the imperial theology of piety, war, victory. In the Roman world, sacrifices were

---

[20] Ellis, "A Note on First Corinthians 10."

political statements about the deification of Caesar and payback for favors, not rituals that would reconcile the people to God's justice-compassion. Because Paul believed that Jesus's death and resurrection were the sign of God's direct action in reclaiming the world for God's Kingdom, and that process would be completed within his lifetime, it would be foolish for people to throw in their lot with the earthly Caesar and participate in the pagan sacrifices.

For reasons known only to the Elves, the rest of 1 Corinthians 10 is never read as part of the Common Lectionary. But look at what Paul is saying in verses 14-22. Paul points out that in the ritual communal meal shared in the community of Christ, the shared cup represents the sacrificial blood of Christ; the broken bread is the risen, transformed body of Christ; "Because there is one bread, we who are many are one body, for we all partake of the one bread." This is mystical language that totally overthrows the civil religious practice of the Roman Empire. And in case his hearers still don't get it, Paul says, "I imply that what pagans [Romans] sacrifice they sacrifice to demons and not to God. . . . You cannot partake of the table of the Lord and the table of demons," or you will "provoke the Lord to jealousy," and break the commandments of God.

Paul's words were subversion in the first century. Are they also subversion in the twenty-first century? Not if the sacrament of communion is seen as the commemoration of Jesus dying in payment (retribution) for the "fall" of humanity.

Perhaps the key is the phrase, "For why should my liberty be subject to the judgment of someone else's conscience?" (1 Cor. 10:29) If we live our lives not out of violent retribution, but by participating in God's justice-compassion, we may indeed end up subverting the law of the land: not deploying with our unit to Iraq; refusing jury duty; donating money to organizations who rescue illegal aliens crossing the border into Texas. But it is the everyday refusal to participate in the prevailing retributive mind-set that will eventually change the paradigm. Speak compassion into the middle of a collective desire for revenge whether it is among family members, neighbors, church committees, or the corporation you work for, and remember Psalm 63, which parallels Paul's faith in God's deliverance for one who lives in the power of God's steadfast love: "My soul is satisfied as with a rich feast. . . but those who seek to destroy my life shall go down into the depths of the earth; they shall be given over to the power of the sword." That's not revenge or retribution. It's the consequence of collusion with Empire.

Spring and the New Moon
Change the Paradigm V:
Fourth Sunday in Lent

Joshua 5:9-12; Psalm 32; 2 Corinthians 5:16-21;
Luke 15:1-3, 11b-32

Frequently the themes of the Common Lectionary readings correspond with what is actually happening in the natural world. It is not surprising that this should be the case, given that the early institutionalized Christian church appropriated pagan festivals wholesale into its liturgical calendar. The conventional interpretation of the readings for today is all about repentance, reconciliation, and forgiveness of sin – in short, new beginnings, starting over, changing focus – matching the metaphors of the new moon, and the spring.

Luke's story of the Prodigal Son is front and center. Everyone knows this story: The younger son takes an early distribution of his portion of the heritage and leaves home, leaving the elder son to his presumed and expected lion's share. The younger son goes off to a far country, and squanders it all on wine, women (presumably), and song. At some point in the middle of this debauchery, when he's spent it all, has maxed out his credit cards, and is reduced to actually working for a living, he comes to his senses and decides to throw himself on the mercy of his family. He offers to take a job tending the pigs, if only his father will give him a place to stay. Much to everyone's surprise – and to the elder son's chagrin – the father is overjoyed at the return of his son. He throws a major party and welcomes him back with open arms. When the elder son objects to this, he is told to deal with it. The son who had died has returned. The one who was lost has been found. Clearly, someone who repents and returns is more valuable than someone who never left in the first place.

In the reading from 2 Cor. 5:16-21, Paul says that from now on we regard no one from a human point of view (i.e., we will not judge based on outside circumstances – such as the debauchery of the prodigal son). Paul writes, "So if anyone is in

Christ, there is a new creation; everything old has passed away; see, everything has become new!" When Paul says "in Christ," the usual interpretation is that we are reconciled to God by the sacrifice of Jesus. God is the reconciler, according to Paul, and the father in Luke's story is the metaphor for that reconciling God. The prodigal son has repented, come home, been reconciled, and has been made new.

End of sermon, right? Time for Sunday dinner, and a nice nap.

Not so fast. The readings once again provide conflicting interpretations of the nature of the God of Israel. Violent/nonviolent.

The Apostle Paul was convinced that Jesus's resurrection was the resurrection of a spiritual, mystical body, which was automatically part of the Kingdom of God – and that we who are living today can also participate in that Kingdom if we choose God's nonviolent distributive justice instead of the violent imperial theology of piety, war, victory. In God's Kingdom of distributive justice, no one is judged by circumstance, but everyone is presumed to be transformed – or at least capable of transformation. Like it or not, the prodigal son's brother learned there is no place in his father's house for payback, for getting even, for locking people up and throwing away the key, for the death penalty. In God's realm of distributive justice the assumption is rehabilitation and hope; in God's realm of distributive justice, the assumption is that everyone has access to power and the assurance of food, clothing, shelter, medical care, and peace regardless of who they are or where they come from.

Paul writes in his second letter to the Corinthians that "there is a new creation: everything old has passed away; see, everything has become new!" John Dominic Crossan suggests "What better deserves the title of a new creation than the abnormalcy of a share-world replacing the normalcy of a greed-world?"[21] Because the coming of God's justice is ongoing – for upwards of 2,000 years now – we are called to participate in a

---

[21]Crossan and Reed, *In Search of Paul,* 176.

new creation– a new paradigm – a world based on letting go, and sharing, rather than keeping and greed.

The moon is new. Spring has begun. For thousands of years, the springtime of the year has been the time when Kings go forth to war. In the passage cherry-picked for this Sunday from the epic saga of Joshua's conquest of Canaan, the Elves leave out the part about how the kings of the Amorites beyond the Jordan to the west, and all the kings of the Canaanites by the sea had been terrified by the drying up of the Jordan that allowed the Israelites to safely invade. Now, the Israelite warriors are freshly circumcised, healed, and ready for rape and plunder. They have eaten their Passover meal of unleavened bread and parched grain possibly stolen from the abandoned farms, so they have no need for God's magic manna. They will plant their own crops and lay claim to the land. Taken in context, it is a violent image that flies in the face of the quiet assurance of Psalm 32, and the courage of faith in the new paradigm that Paul and Jesus before him gave their lives for.

We can choose which God we will follow: The god of violence, pillage, war, greed – Imperial power that declares opponents and adversaries "enemy combatants" at best and inhuman at worst; that ignores evidence of the adverse effects of misuse of the earth in a paradigm of conquest and dominion – or the *kenotic,* non-interventionist God that Jesus pointed to, and that Paul ecstatically recognized.

Now is the time to make that choice – in our families, work groups, communities. That's what repentance really means. Turning around. Changing direction. Choosing to participate in the new paradigm: Covenant, nonviolence, justice-compassion, and peace.

The Woman with the Alabaster Jar
Change the Paradigm VI:
Fifth Sunday in Lent

*Isaiah 43:16-21; Psalm 126; Philippians 3:4b-14; John 12:1-8
(cf. Mark 14:1-11)*

The story of the woman with the alabaster jar is so
powerful that it appears in all the gospels. Therefore, to my
mind, the incident may very well have actually happened. The
question is when, and under what circumstances. She must have
been an important member – even a leader – in Jesus's
entourage, even though she is unnamed in Mark, Matthew, and
Luke. John assumes she was Mary, the sister of Martha and
Lazarus, close friends of Jesus. Mark, Matthew, and John place
the story in Jesus's last days as he journeys toward Jerusalem,
death, and resurrection. In Luke's version she is a penitent
prostitute (by legend, Mary Magdalene), and the story is treated
as a scandal. The Elves have selected the version in John's
Gospel for the Fifth Sunday in Lent. Consider along with that
the version in Mark 14:1-11, discussed in depth by Marcus
Borg and John Dominic Crossan in *The Last Week*.[22]

As Jesus and the twelve and the rest of the followers
journey from Caesarea Philippi to Jerusalem, Jesus tries on
three occasions to convince the twelve that to be first in the
Kingdom of God means giving personal power away, or using
personal power-with and for another as a servant or slave or
child, not political or personal power-over others. To follow
Jesus's way means to participate with him in bringing about
God's justice-compassion – the nonviolent alternative to Roman
imperial violence. He warns constantly that to do that means to
follow him into and through death itself. He will be captured,
tortured, and killed because his message attracts the people, and
offers a direct threat to the authority of the Roman occupiers.
Indeed, the writer of John's Gospel tells us in 12:9 that ". . . the
chief priests planned to put Lazarus to death as well, since it

---

[22]Borg and Crossan, *The Last Week*, 85-107.

69

was on account of him that many of the [people] were deserting and were believing in Jesus."

Mark assures his hearers that Jesus will be resurrected on the third day. Much in the same way as we enjoy the story of Romeo and Juliette, Mark's audience can be assured that the triumph comes, and Jesus wins eternal life in the end. But the disciples don't believe Jesus. Just as it was unthinkable that God would allow his temple to be destroyed, so it was unthinkable that God would allow his Messiah to be defeated. The disciples ignore the gathering political storm clouds, and imagine themselves sharing the glorious victory. They don't get the paradigm shift Jesus is insisting on. They can't see their way out of the prevailing normalcy of imperial, hierarchical rule. Judas makes the ultimate betrayal, literally selling Jesus to the Romans, in John's version of the story, which makes Judas into an ordinary thief or robber, interested in his own selfish agenda, rather than one who is simply unable to give up his identification with the normalcy of Roman rule, and the paradigm of hierarchy and power-over.

In Mark's version of the story the unnamed woman is the only one who gets Jesus's message. She alone hears and believes his certainty that his body will need to be prepared for burial. It is the final service that can be done for anyone; it was the job of women to do it; and she will not have another chance to do so. In a demonstration of the kind of servant-leadership that Jesus kept trying to get the disciples to understand, she takes a jar of perfume – which cost at least a year's wages – and pours it over Jesus's head. In John's version, she washes Jesus's feet with it, and dries them with her hair – a dramatic and startling act of total submission and hospitality, and John's Jesus acknowledges this. Mark has Jesus say, "Truly I tell you, wherever the good news is proclaimed in the whole world, what she has done will be told in remembrance of her." These words are similar to the familiar words of institution of the Lord's Supper in Luke's later gospel: "Do this in remembrance of me" (Luke 22:19). But by the time Luke was writing, of course, the early church had aligned itself with the normalcy of Roman rule, and the woman with the alabaster jar was reduced from prophetic leader to a common and insignificant sinner.

Paul's letter to the Philippians claims that Paul himself has given up everything so that he can participate with the risen Christ, *not* with imperial rule: "For his sake I have suffered the loss of all things, and I regard them as rubbish, in order that I may be found in him, not having a righteousness of my own that comes from the law, but one that comes through faith in Christ, the righteousness from God based on faith." Then Paul once more waxes passionate: ". . . if somehow I may attain the resurrection from the dead[,] not that I have already obtained this or have already reached the goal; . . . I do not consider that I have made it my own; but this one thing I do: forgetting what lies behind and straining forward to what lies ahead, I press on toward the goal for the prize of the heavenly call of God in Christ Jesus." Paul is convinced, he *knows* that God's justice-compassion is coming, its institution is inevitable. To think that the Kingdom will not come is impossible for Paul because with Jesus's death and resurrection, the process had already begun. God was already taking direct action to restore justice-compassion in the world. In Crossan's words, "God's great clean-up had begun."

If the writer of Mark was aware of Paul's theology, the story of the woman with the alabaster jar becomes profound, as she prepares Jesus's earthly body in advance for the transformed spiritual body, raised as the first fruits of those martyrs who died in the service of God's justice-compassion. She is already participating with Jesus in the establishment of God's Kingdom on earth, here and now. Who knows what the circumstances were that produced the original action on the part of that unnamed woman in Jesus's company? Who knows what the gesture might have meant, if she did it two (Mark) or six (John) days before Passover of the week Jesus died? From the twenty-first century point of view, it is a declaration of solidarity, and willingness to see Jesus through whatever the Roman occupiers might like to subject him to. A far cry from the response of the perhaps willfully blind twelve, who pay him lip service, then desert him at the first opportunity. And we of course, would never do such a thing . . . . At least Mark's Judas is honest. He can't believe Jesus's way can possibly work, so he abandons the company and turns Jesus in to the authorities.

71

This interpretation of the story is an indictment of twenty-first century "believers" who reduce Jesus's death and resurrection to payment for individual petty sin. The story is also an indictment of twenty-first century "believers" who ignore the injustice inherent in the imperial air we breathe every day. Just like the twelve, we cannot see the difference between leadership and tyranny; we cannot see the difference between accountability and retribution; wealth, physical strength, ability to persuade, age, gender, social class, religion, race – all the different expressions of humanity – become hierarchical qualifications that determine access to power and the opportunity to survive.

But we have the power, at any moment, to transform the way we live our lives. We can choose not to participate in the retributive system of imperial war and systemic injustice. We can step into the kind of ongoing parallel universe of God's justice-compassion at any moment. We can change our consciousness, change the paradigm in which we live, whenever we have the will to do so. And when the rare opportunity presents itself, we can break the alabaster jar in remembrance of her.

Easter

Transformation
Easter Sunday

Acts 10:34-43; 1 Corinthians 15:19-26; John 20:1-18

Of course the tomb is empty. Jesus is risen as the Christ. The fear of death and its power have been overcome. If the tomb had not been empty, none of the rest of the history of the Western world would have happened. Does that mean that the man Jesus literally walked out of the grave as a resuscitated zombie corpse? Of course not. That is the stuff of unnatural horror. What is natural and wondrous is the power of personal transformation from participation in the usual systems of imperial injustice to the *kenotic* selflessness of changing consciousness at will and stepping into the realm of God's justice-compassion.

If only it were as easy as that. But if it were, we would not be human, and the evolution of the Christ consciousness from the terror of self-realization after the primordial seamlessness of Eden's being would not have been necessary.

"If for this life only we have hoped in Christ, we are of all people most to be pitied. But in fact Christ has been raised from the dead, the first fruits of those who have died. For since death came through a human being, the resurrection of the dead has also come through a human being; for as all die in Adam, so all will be made alive in Christ . . . the last enemy to be destroyed is death," sings the Apostle Paul.

Those who are unable or unwilling to participate in the Christ consciousness – the Kingdom of God's distributive justice-compassion – live in loveless terror. At any given moment in the history of humankind, those "sinners" seem to hold sway. Loveless terror is just as likely as justice-compassion to be resurrected from the tomb of human consciousness. The job of the enlightened – the "elect" – the "chosen" – is to spend ourselves without counting the cost in saving the ones still trapped in darkness, chained to the rotting corpse.

Living the Metaphor Part I:
Four Questions for the Apocalypse
Second Sunday in Eastertide

Acts 5:27-32: Psalm 118:14-29; Revelation 1:4-8;
John 20:19-31

The Easter Season has begun. Now the traditional dogma of the Church is reinforced with the stories from the Acts of the Apostles, written by the writer of Luke, and the theology of the writer of the Gospel of John and of Revelation. It is important to realize that in all likelihood, none of the stories about Jesus's appearances in John, nor the adventures of the Apostles in Acts are history remembered; none of the sayings of John's Jesus can be traced directly back to him; and the Revelation to John (Apocalypse) is an extended allegory reiterating the conviction that God will act directly and violently in human history to restore God's retributive justice to earth. Apparently the creators of the RCL decided that the Revelation to John is a "prophecy," and have substituted it for the usual reading from the Old Testament prophets. Unfortunately, "prophecy" among the literalists means a foretelling of future events, not a crystallization of insight about where current events may be taking us.

When considering the readings for this season in Year C, the underlying framework for these commentaries must be revisited: Is the nature of God violent or nonviolent? Is Jesus's message inclusive or exclusive? Does faith require the suspension of disbelief or commitment to the great work of justice-compassion? Does deliverance mean salvation from hell or liberation from injustice?

This first series of Eastertide readings traditionally illustrates violence, exclusion, suspension of disbelief, and salvation from hell. Jesus walks through closed doors and chastises Thomas for demanding physical proof that Jesus is alive; Peter and the leadership of the Jewish Christians in Jerusalem continue their confrontation with the Temple authorities who collaborated with Rome. They refuse to stop teaching forgiveness of sins in the name of Jesus and holding the Temple authorities accountable for Jesus's death. The writer of Revelation claims that Jesus is coming again to the dismay of "all of the tribes of earth."

What do post-enlightenment, postmodern minds do with this other than throw it out?

The mystics among us can come into the conversation at this point. Classically, a mystic is a person who is comfortable in a non-rational existence; one who finds truth beyond the physical, provable realms. In short, a mystic is someone who lives in the metaphor. The trick is to live in the metaphor without making it literal. That is the only way to avoid the trap of missing Jesus's message – not to mention sightings of Elvis and the Blessed Virgin.

A postmodern mystic might look at this week's appearance story in John as a realization of the truth of the empty tomb: Jesus's spirit is alive. Further, in an echo of God's action in Genesis, Jesus breathes on the apostles and says "As the Father has sent me, so I send you. Receive the Holy Spirit. If you forgive the sins of any, they are forgiven them; if you retain the sins of any, they are retained." But rather than empowering every person to live the life that Jesus lived in communion with the Kingdom of God, this great commission has become a frightening and dangerous barrier that continues to exclude undesirables of all ages, races, genders, and circumstances. The mystical apostolic succession has been established. The apostles meeting in John's closed room have become magicians who control the power. Only the lucky ones who receive the Holy Spirit from Jesus's representatives in the Christian community have the power to forgive sins, or to withhold forgiveness. This is not history remembered, it is first century metaphor literalized.

Not everyone is a mystic. Some require a graphic vision to grasp the spiritual reality, and Thomas the Doubter is one. Jesus gives him his physical proof and says, "Blessed are those who have not seen and yet have come to believe." Does that mean Thomas is a pig-headed skeptic, and that those who "have faith" are somehow more deserving of salvation from sin? The accompanying reading from Revelation implies that the skeptics

77

will be quickly culled from the believers as soon as Jesus comes again "with the clouds; every eye will see him, even those who pierced him; and on his account all the tribes of the earth will wail."

The Acts of the Apostles has a lot of mystical stuff in it – angels, magical openings of prisons, blinding flashes of transforming visions, etc., but they are all told as though they are history remembered. Luke – or whatever the name of the Greek was who wrote both Luke and Acts – seems to be writing for the literalists in the early Christian community. Peter and "the apostles" with him seem to delight in sticking it to the Temple authorities, claiming "We must obey God, not any human authority . . . and we are witnesses to these things, and so is the Holy Spirit, whom God has given to those who obey him" and not to *you*. Nyah Nyah Nyah."

Later in the story (which is not included by the Elves for study or illumination of the text) somebody in the "council" stands up and says, "If this plan or this undertaking is of human origin, it will fail; but if it is of God, you will not be able to overthrow them – in that case, you may even be found fighting against God!" This is a practical first century voice. It is also a warning against anyone who opposes Peter's *and Luke's* interpretation of Jesus's message. Peter's reported action in Acts is violent because it claims exclusivity and privilege. Therefore, Peter's God is a violent God; Peter's Jesus is exclusive; and suspension of disbelief is the order of the day, not participation with the risen Christ in actualizing God's justice-compassion in the world. Deliverance in this context means salvation from the consequences of personal sin, not liberation from injustice. Again, the accompanying "prophecy" of Revelation is that, in a violent and unjust world, controlled by a violent, interventionist God, Jesus is on his way back to terrorize the tribes of earth who, even though they might see, do not believe.

So back to the questions: 1) What is the nature of God? Violent or nonviolent? 2) What is the nature of Jesus's message? Inclusive or exclusive? 3)What is faith? Suspension of disbelief or commitment to the great work of justice-compassion? 4) What is deliverance? Salvation from hell or liberation from injustice?

Curiously, the Elves have suggested Psalm 118:14-29 as the accompanying liturgy of praise. There is not a word of retribution in the entire Psalm. Perhaps somewhere, someone realized that all of the vignettes in today's readings can be interpreted as nonviolent, inclusive, commitment to the great work of justice-compassion in partnership with the Christ consciousness that brings liberation from injustice.

Jesus's true message needs to be reclaimed.

Living the Metaphor Part II:
The Eschaton Continues
Third Sunday in Eastertide

Acts 9:1-20: Psalm 30; Revelation 5:11-14; John 21:1-19

The orthodox interpretation for this week's readings begins with Revelation. The mighty chorus from Part II of Handel's Messiah rings in our minds. Mightier, perhaps, than the famous Hallelujah Chorus, because it lays out the entire 1,800-year theology of the Christian world of Handel's time, and little has changed in the last 200 years:

Worthy is the Lamb that was slain,
and has redeemed us to God by his blood
to receive power and riches and wisdom and strength
and honor and glory and blessing.
Blessing and honor, glory and power be unto him
who sits on the throne and unto the Lamb forever and ever.

The rest of the readings are heard in that context. A violent God has violently intervened to redeem sinners with the blood of the purest, unblemished sacrifice – the son of God himself – and thereby, all humanity receives power and riches and wisdom and strength and honor and glory and blessing. To the victor go the spoils. Onward Christian soldiers. Oh yeah. "Blessing and honor, glory and power be unto *him*" as well, "forever and ever." But no riches, wisdom, or strength. Those are human needs. The Christ is devoid of humanity (*kenosis*).

Likewise Saul of Tarsus is struck down by the risen Jesus, and remains blinded for three days, after which he is healed by a disciple (Ananais) in Damascus, and ordained – commissioned – by that disciple to take Jesus's message to the gentiles. Saul replicates the death and resurrection of Jesus, and Jesus himself tells Ananais that "I myself will show him [Saul] how much he must suffer for the sake of my name." More violence, this time from and for the message of Jesus.

The appearance story in John's Gospel is a favorite. Peter and the guys are fishing, and not having much luck. A man onshore calls out to them and tells them to put their nets on the right side of the boat. Immediately, there are so many fish that their nets will scarcely hold them. Peter (the impetuous one) puts his clothes *back on* (a curiously puritanical or pious act), jumps into the water, and swims to shore to greet Jesus. So that there is no mistake as to the identity of the magician on the shore, Jesus breaks bread, blesses the fish, and distributes the meal. Then three times Jesus demands that Peter acknowledge that he loves Jesus, and commands him to "feed my sheep." Having made up for denying Jesus three times on the night he was arrested by the Romans, Peter learns that he will die a violent death – but we already knew that, because Paul got the same bad news.

The possibilities for literal mayhem in these stories are infinite:

- The sacraments (conferring exclusivity): *Baptism:* Saul receives the Holy Spirit from Ananais and is baptized once his sight is restored; Peter jumps into the water (immersion). *Ordination*: Ananais lays hands on Saul and commissions him at Jesus's command; Peter is commissioned three times to tend the sheep left behind by Jesus himself. *Communion:* Saul takes some food after his baptism; Peter and the others receive bread and fish from Jesus's own hands.
- Martyrdom (the violence accompanying Jesus's message): Both Peter and Saul are shown that their lives will end violently in the service of Jesus's message.
- Atonement (the violence of God): ransom or substitution.
- Miraculous deliverance (from sin): Jesus tells the fishermen to lower their nets on the *right* side – the correct side? The politically expedient side? Why not the *left*?

Keeping in mind the questions for this season, is there any meaning to these stories that is a nonviolent, inclusive, commitment to justice-compassion, and liberation from injustice?

Again, the Psalm choice provides some balance. Psalm 30 is a psalm of praise for recovery from illness. Illness may be metaphorically understood as an indication of being estranged from God. The psalmist sings of going from security and prosperity to near death, and being delivered by God. The Psalmist says that when "I cried to you for help, . . . you have healed me . . . you have turned my mourning into dancing; you have taken off my sackcloth and clothed me with joy." Suppose this Psalm, possibly dating to 164 B.C.E., is really closer to the historical Jesus's understanding of the nonviolent nature of God and God's Kingdom than to the interpreters of Jesus's story, writing from 90 to 125 years after Jesus's death. Using Psalm 30 as the grounding theology instead of Revelation can transform the meaning of these stories into hope for deliverance as the followers of Jesus prepare to take his message of Covenant, nonviolence, justice, and peace into the dangerous first and second century Roman world. Twenty centuries later, the eschaton continues, and the choices remain: Violence or nonviolence; Inclusion or exclusion; Suspension of disbelief or commitment to the great work of justice-compassion; Salvation from hell or liberation from injustice.

Living the Metaphor Part III:
Crimes against Divinity
Fourth Sunday in Eastertide

Acts 9:36-43; Psalm 23; Revelation 7:9-17; John 10:22-30

The reading from The Revelation of John so completely reflects Psalm 23 that the orthodox sermon practically writes itself. Traditionally, these stories confirm the patriarchal power of the Church for miraculous healing; confirm that the Lord is the shepherd who will bring his flock safely to heaven after the great violent overthrow of Satan; and remind us that "the Jews" refuse to believe what is physically proven to them by Jesus's own works because they are not part of the flock that belongs to Jesus, to whom he has given eternal life and safety. Jesus is God. The heresy – indeed the crime against divinity – of the exclusion of Jews from God's Kingdom, which is committed to this day by fundamentalists, becomes ever more solid.

Dorcas (or Tabitha) is the only woman in the entire New Testament who is referred to with the feminine form of the word "disciple." From the point of view of postmodern feminist theology, this woman was so powerful, even Luke was forced to acknowledge her with not one Aramaic name, but the Greek translation as well. The name means "gazelle" – which is one of the smallest and most graceful of the family of deer. So not only was Dorcas a respected leader in the early Christian community in Joppa, she was well known for her skill as a seamstress, and to top it all off, she was likely physically beautiful. Too much for poor, patriarchal Luke. Dorcas – the powerful woman disciple – has to die and be resurrected by Peter. When she wakes up, she sits up on her own, but then Peter takes her hand and helps her to stand. In contrast, earlier, in the section left out by the Elves (Acts 9:32-35), the story about Peter in Lydda has Peter telling a bedridden, paralyzed man named Aeneas to get up and walk. Aeneas – who is not a disciple – needs no further help from Peter. Behind these miracles is a second crime against divinity: the subtle indication of the misogynist violence that has historically plagued the institutional Church.

We may not be able to reclaim any of the metaphors offered in this week's readings. The stories about Peter will have to be discarded, unless faith means the suspension of disbelief that the lame shall walk and the dead shall be raised. Suspension of disbelief is the only option for John's Jesus, who is clear about who belongs to him and who does not. Nor is there any redemption to be found in the Revelation chapter. The only way for the "great multitude . . . from every nation, from all tribes and peoples and languages" to participate in God's ultimate Kingdom is by violent purification through the "blood of the Lamb."

Again, the Psalm offers the alternative peaceable kingdom, even though its meaning is corrupted by its association with the other readings. So we are left once more with the choices: The violence or nonviolence of God; whether Jesus's message is inclusive or exclusive; faith as suspension of disbelief or commitment to the great work of justice-compassion; and deliverance as salvation from hell or liberation from injustice.

This week the odds are with the normalcy of civilization: violence, exclusion, suspension of disbelief, and salvation from hell – in other words, piety, war, victory – and uneasy peace.

Pentecost

Genesis 11:1-9; Acts 2:1-2; Psalm 104; Romans 8:14-17; John 14:8-17, 25-27

Old Paradigm (Christian Orthodoxy):

God prevents humans from speaking the same language because, as God makes clear in Genesis 2, humans must not be allowed to be like God – knowing good and evil, and able to create life in their own image. But no matter what God tried, humans kept on "sinning." So God sent Jesus as a last resort, and to underscore the point, allowed the "sinners" to kill him. "Pentecost" is celebrated as the birthday of the Christian church. Nationwide, the verses from Acts 2:1-13 will be read in as many languages as can be cobbled together by graduates of high school language classes from family Bibles of refugees and immigrants, all to celebrate the "universality" of the message that Jesus died to save humanity from sin and death. So long as humans believe that Jesus died to save them from sin, Jesus and the Holy Spirit will do whatever humans ask of them, because the spirit of Jesus and the Holy Spirit are in humans, and humans (who believe in Jesus) are in the Holy Spirit. Therefore, nothing they ask Jesus to do for them can possibly be evil. Humans are the adopted children of God, and stand to inherit God's Kingdom so long as humans also suffer as Jesus did.

New Paradigm (Postmodern Liberal Christianity):

Psalm 104 flies in the face of the petty jealousy of the God of Genesis 11. Psalm 104 says, God is just, and the world belongs to God. There is no need for God to intervene and scramble the minds of humankind in order to prevent them from accruing too much power. God provides "springs to gush forth in the valleys . . . grass to grow for the cattle . . . plants for people to use . . . and wine to gladden the human heart." In God's Kingdom, humanity is a partner, working to restore God's justice-compassion to a world ("flesh") that sets its mind on self-interest ("the things of the flesh"). When humanity works together with the spirit of God to restore God's justice-compassion, then all are children of God, and heirs to the Kingdom of justice-compassion, even if we lose our physical lives in the process.

Reducing these readings to screeds about "sexual sin" or personal petty trespass is a travesty. So is believing literally that Jesus will do whatever Christians ask of him – which has meant devastating crusades in search of "victory," nationalistic narcissism, the wholesale eradication of indigenous peoples world wide, and ultimately the threatened destruction of the Planet itself.

It is patently unfair to the spirit of the Apostle Paul to cherry-pick individual verses out of the context of the pivotal letter to the Romans. Chapter 8 should be read in its entirety – or at least verses 1-13 along with 14-17. Instead of the word "flesh," substitute the word "self-interest," and instead of the word "righteousness" substitute "justice-compassion." Then Paul's argument begins to come into focus:

"But you are not subject to self-interest. You are in the Spirit, since the Spirit of God dwells in you . . . . If Christ is in you, even though life is meaningless because of collaboration with the forces of Empire, the Spirit is life because of justice-compassion . . . . So then, brothers and sisters, we are in debt – not to self-interest, to live according to self-interest, because if you do that, your life becomes meaningless – but if by the Spirit you abandon self-interest, you will have abundant life. You did not receive a spirit of slavery to the laws of Empire, but you were adopted by God to be children and joint heirs with Christ of God's Kingdom of justice-compassion."

Paul's letter is an inspiration – a call to faith in the power of the spirit of justice-compassion for freedom and abundance, not a condemnation of human weakness and an attempt to control human thought and action. Indeed, the first words of Chapter 8 are, "There is therefore now no condemnation for those who are in Christ Jesus, for the law of the spirit of life in Christ Jesus has set you free from the law of collaboration with injustice and death. For God has done what the law – weakened by self-interest – could not do." God sent the Christ to show us how to deal with the struggle between violence and nonviolence; between retributive justice and distributive justice-

86

compassion; between collaboration with Empire – the prevailing normalcy of retributive justice – and abandoning self-interest to join the great work of justice-compassion.

Season after Pentecost
(Ordinary Time)

Sophia Logos Charis
Trinity Sunday

Proverbs 8:1-4, 22-3; Psalm 8; Romans 5:1-5; John 16:12-15

In the continuing argument in these essays about participating with God in restoring God's distributive justice-compassion to a world that prefers the normalcy of imperial retributive justice, comes this amazing combination of readings for Trinity Sunday. "Trinity" in Christian dogma usually means "Father, Son and Holy Ghost"; and using John's "spirit of truth" as the "holy ghost" we have a thoroughly masculine trinity. But the readings suggest a different balance: Wisdom/Sophia – the Divine Feminine – was the first creation of God's work, according to the Wisdom tradition in Proverbs 8. John's Word (the Spirit of Truth that "will guide you into all the truth") is definitely the masculine "logos," and the third aspect, the "grace in which we stand" is the free gift (*charis*) of God, from which nothing can separate us because we have been *made just* – "justified" – by faith in God's justice-compassion, and not by the works of the law.

The Wisdom reading pulls us into the origins of the universe itself. Out of the mysterious Wisdom of the Cosmos, the universe was born. In *The Universe Story*, Brian Swimme and Thomas Berry illustrate the intertwining of Word and Wisdom – Logos and Sophia:

> Without a sensitivity to primordial communication within the universe, the universe's story comes to an end. That this is certainly the case with an individual organism we can readily appreciate in the case of the monarch butterfly. Climbing out of the pupal shell, stretching its wings in the drying sunlight, what other than the voices of the universe can that butterfly rely upon for guidance? It must make a journey that will cover territory filled with both dangers and possibilities, none of which has ever been experienced before. To rely on its own personal experience or knowledge

would be a disaster for the butterfly. Instead it finds itself surrounded by voices of the past, of the other insects, of the wind and the rain and the leaves of the trees.

The information of the genetic material comes forth precisely within its interactions. That is, the monarch butterfly has little if any individual awareness of the difference between beneficial winds and dangerous winds until it finds itself confronted by them in reality. The winds speak to the butterfly, the taste of the water speaks to the butterfly, the shape of the leaf speaks to the butterfly and offers a guidance that resonates with the wisdom coded into the butterfly's being. Such communication takes place beneath the level of language, even that of genetic language. It functions at the primordial reality of primal contact. The source of the guidance is both within and without . . .[23]

The butterfly lives in a seamless realm, a matrix, poetically in the palm of God/dess's hand, not alien or estranged. Suppose we try looking at the fields of flowers and the full moon, and the wheels in wheels of galaxies? Try lying flat on your back in your yard on a starry summer night and consider you are looking down instead of up. After the dizziness passes, you may begin to realize the wisdom and power of gravity. Or watch a bird's nest attached to a branch during a storm and consider the wisdom and power of riding the wind.

The readings are calling us to look and listen to what God's creation is telling us. Aboriginal people ("first" people – native people) seem to have a better handle on how to do that than most members of Western civilization. The problem is, Western Christians may spend a weekend retreat studying "Native American spirituality" or "Celtic Christianity," but the concepts aren't often really learned and put to use. Instead, ideas of a great balance among the various life forms in the natural world, or aligning oneself with the four directions (or seven), or

---

[23]Swimme and Berry, *The Universe Story*, 42.

meeting in a circle become a romantic interlude most suitable for special services put on by youth groups. Once the retreat or the special service is over, we get back to what we know will save us, which is orthodox belief. Except we really don't believe it.

We live in a postmodern world. Fear and uncertainty are the order of the day. Somehow the concept of "grace" (*charis* – "free gift") has become anything but "free." The Church has insisted that "grace" is bestowed only on believers, who are therefore "saved" from hell and eternal death. The price of "salvation" is all too often suspension of disbelief in the triple-decker universe and the resuscitation of a corpse. Worse, while no statistics are provided, "the dark side of absolute certainty about faith seem(s) to be a deep, restless self-questioning."[24] The Church teaches us from the cradle that nothing we do can assure us that we are indeed saved – maybe because we suspect somewhere deep in our hearts that we're really only a breath away from evil – one step from the precipice of the "straight and narrow" into perdition.

Didn't Jesus die once and for all? Apparently, many Christians don't believe their own theology.

What if the Apostle Paul had it right? Suppose that nothing indeed can separate us from the love of God? To paraphrase Paul later on in Romans: So now abide Wisdom, Word, and Grace – these three – and perhaps the greatest of these is Grace. If we know that nothing can separate us from the love of God, we can then step into the great work of justice-compassion without fear. It's not about doing fabulous things to great acclaim. It's about changing consciousness from retribution and guilt to fairness and love. Paul never says this is easy. He says, we know "that suffering produces endurance, and endurance produces character, and character produces hope, and hope does not disappoint us because God's love has been poured into our hearts through the Holy Spirit that has been *given* to us."

It's embarrassing to be given something we think we haven't earned or don't deserve. And it's even worse to observe the gift bestowed upon someone we know doesn't deserve it

---

[24]Johnson Frykholm, "Reading the Rapture."

because we think they haven't done the work, or don't follow the belief system.

Get over it.

Wisdom delights in humanity, which Psalm 8 tells us has dominion over the works of God's hand: the beasts of the field, the birds of the air, and the fish of the sea. We know that God is just, and the world belongs to God. So if we look around at our human stewardship of God's creation, and we see injustice and death, then it is up to us to set things right.

Proper 5
A Different Gospel?

*1 Kings 17:8-24; Psalm 146; Psalm 30; Galatians 1:11-24;
Luke 7:11-17*

When the movable feast for Easter causes the elimination
of Proper 4, we pick up Paul's letter to the Galatians at 1:11
instead of at the beginning. This allows for continued cherry-
picking and missing the point of Paul's interpretation of Jesus's
message, and Paul's reason for his angry and almost despairing
diatribe against the pagan community in Galatia, which he had
converted to the new Christianity.

There is plenty in the readings to satisfy orthodoxy. The
great Elijah saga in 1 and 2 Kings also runs along with Luke
and Galatians for the next several Sundays. In the Proper 5
readings, Elijah first saves the poor widow of Zarephath from
starvation, then raises her son from the dead. In Luke chapter
7:1-17, Jesus remotely heals a Roman centurion's slave, then
raises the widow's son at Nain. Clearly, Luke claims, Jesus is
the new Elijah. His credentials are impeccable. Speaking of
credentials (from the orthodox point of view), Paul's credentials
as an evangelist for Christ are also impeccable: "'The one who
formerly was persecuting us is now proclaiming the faith he
once tried to destroy,'" quotes Paul to the Galatians, "And they
glorified God because of me." We of course should go and do
likewise. It's a clear call to mission, healing, even raising the
dead.

But what's really going on?

In order to find that out, we need to read the notes written
by Richard B. Hays in *The Harper Collins Study Bible* – as a
minimum – and then consider Paul's mission in the context of
first century Roman imperial hegemony, as suggested by
scholars such as John Dominic Crossan and Marcus J. Borg.
The letter to the Galatian Christian community reflects a
continuing need for Paul to explain that Jesus's death and
resurrection was the sign that – in Crossan's words – God's
great clean-up of the world from imperial injustice and
retribution to God's Kingdom of justice-compassion had begun.

The new covenant with God is not one of imperial human normalcy contained in human law, but the agreement to participate with God's free gift of grace in the ongoing program of distributive justice-compassion. Ten years after this letter, Paul's struggle to keep Jesus's message from being corrupted by the collaborators with Empire culminated with his final essay on sin and the law written to the Christian community in Rome itself.

In Paul's view, because of their compromise with the organizers of the Christians in Jerusalem to comply with Jewish circumcision as a sign of God's covenant, the community he had founded in Galatia had opted for violence, exclusiveness, literal belief, and salvation from hell. Law – whether Roman or Jewish – is the foundation for sin in Paul's view. Even more important, Jesus's death in the service of restoring God's justice-compassion on earth mandated God's free gift of grace with no need for any proof through the law of participation with God's Kingdom of justice-compassion. To opt for even a small part of Jewish law meant that the Galatians had rejected God's free gift of grace, and had sold out to the imperial gospel of religion (piety), war, victory, and promises of peace – and the struggle continues today

Throughout the Bible, including the New Testament, these four questions hold the tension between the nonviolent God's distributive justice-compassion, and the violent God's exclusive retribution. The Elijah story is about faith in God's distributive justice. In exchange for extending hospitality to God's servant Elijah – and thereby choosing to participate in God's promised Kingdom of justice-compassion – the widow's jar of meal will not empty, nor the jug of oil fail until the day the Lord sends rain (justice) upon the earth. When the widow's son falls ill, seemingly in contradiction to God's promised justice, Elijah demands that God be true to himself.

The Luke story is about inclusiveness as well as justice. Jesus recognizes distributive justice even in a Roman centurion, who respects Jesus's authority and the Jewish tradition, and asks him to heal his slave. Luke's Jesus comments that not even in Israel has he seen the kind of faith in God's distributive justice as was evident in the pagan Roman centurion. Faith, in

96

both of these traditional stories, means trust in a nonviolent God whose distributive justice-compassion holds sway in an unjust world.

There *is* another gospel, as Paul scathingly points out. It is the one where God is violent, Jesus's message is exclusive, literal belief is the litmus test, and salvation means deliverance from hell. The people want easy answers and cheap grace. But the price for "pleasing people" with easy answers and cheap grace results in a theology of uncertainty, self-doubt, and fear, requiring strict control over thought and behavior – i.e., law. Paul's experience is that the power of sin itself is found in the law, because the law codifies and restricts without compromise, which inevitably results either in injustice, or in the necessity to break the law, and thereby be guilty of sin.

That other gospel produces a church that persists in preaching sin in this life and redemption in the next based on belief, rather than a gospel of grace – free gift – *charis* – for all who choose to participate in this life in the great work of justice-compassion. The result too often is a belief system with monstrous consequences: a prominent right-wing "Christian" religious leader declares that the terrible events in the United States of September 11, 2001, were God's punishment of a decadent society; a child dies in an accidental apartment fire, and the mother – beyond grief – says that God wanted another angel.

Paul wastes no time. As soon as he steps over the Galatian threshold with grace and peace, he starts in: "I am astonished that you are so quickly deserting the one who called you in the grace of Christ and are turning to a different gospel – not that there *is* another gospel, but there are some who are confusing you and want to pervert the gospel of Christ . . . . [I]f anyone proclaims to you a gospel contrary to what you received, let that one be accursed!" And he repeats the curse, to assure that there is no question about where he stands on the issue. "Am I now seeking human approval, or God's approval?" he demands. "[In other words], am I trying to please people? If I were still pleasing people, I would not be a servant of Christ."

Light the fire. The man is not going to recant.

97

Proper 6
Outside, Not Above, the Law

1 Kings 21:1-21; 2 Samuel 11:26-12:10, 13-15; Galatians 2:15-21; Luke 7:36-8:3; Psalm 5:1-8; Psalm 32

This week's theme contains at least three levels of spiritual struggle.

On one level we see human egos that are only interested in their own gratification. In the story from 1 Kings, Ahab's queen, Jezebel, organizes a campaign to kill Naboth, who owns a vineyard coveted by Ahab. Ahab thus is in violation of three of the Ten Commandments: you shall not covet your neighbor's house and goods; you shall not bear false witness against another; and you shall not kill. In the second reading, the creators of the RCL bring us in at the end of King David's arranged murder of Uriah so that he can take Uriah's wife Bathsheba for himself. Covetousness and murder are the order of the day.

On another level, we have cosmic justice-compassion contrasted with the normalcy of imperial retributive justice. Paul preaches in Romans that "the strength of sin is the law." Various interpretations of that phrase have been perpetrated over the millennia, but generally it is incomprehensible so long as "sin" means petty trespass. However, the stories of Kings Ahab and David are not only about petty trespass, using the law – the authority of the King – to accomplish selfish ends and feed bully egos. These abuses of power break trust with the people on three levels: David and Ahab betray their own integrity, confound the laws of the land, and break the laws of God.

The prophet Nathan speaks on behalf of God for both stories, as far as the Elves are concerned. He tells a story about blatant injustice, and when David is rightly outraged, declares "You are the man!" If we read on in the Elijah saga and complete Ahab's story, we find that both Nathan and Elijah essentially "forgive" their respective Kings because they repent of their sin. The prophets exact the payment anyway from future generations, perhaps because these are not just petty trespasses, but cosmic breaches of sovereign trust.

There is a difference between the short-term forgiveness extended to Ahab and David with the retribution exacted by God from future generations, and the free gift of grace (cosmic forgiveness) won by the death of Jesus and extended to all who accept the invitation to the great work of justice-compassion.

Paul is reminding the Galatians that if they accept the risen Christ as their Lord, they must reject the imperial rule of law, whether it is Jewish or Roman. Otherwise, Paul says, "Christ died for nothing." Well then, the Galatians apparently argued, if we reject the law, but still sin – perhaps as Ahab and David did –"is Christ then a servant of sin?" Don't be ridiculous, Paul says. If I reconstruct the unjust retributive imperial system after dismantling it, then I am indeed a transgressor because I have betrayed the Christ who reconciled me with God's justice-compassion. We are justified not by adherence to law, but by acknowledging the death of Jesus as an invitation to participate in restoring God's justice-compassion to the world, and choosing to accept that invitation. When we accept that invitation, we are made just because we become coworkers with God in that great work of justice-compassion, not co-workers with unjust imperial rule.

Finally, we cannot ignore the women in these readings. They are all named women, which means they were powerful and well-known, whether they were actual historical people or not.

In Luke's hands, the story of the woman with the alabaster jar of ointment becomes a story about hospitality, but it may also be an attempt to convey the idea of grace. Luke has Jesus say that "her sins, which were many, have been forgiven; hence (therefore) she has shown great love." Is Luke saying that when one is forgiven, then one is able to love extravagantly (grace)? Contrary to Paul's teaching, Luke seems to put a value on how much "grace" one receives from the forgiveness of sins. "The one to whom little is forgiven loves little." Was Mary Magdalene the woman with the alabaster jar? Does Luke mean that Mary Magdalene loved the most because, as he reports later, "seven demons had gone out" from her? Is Paul's argument about the free gift of grace already so totally misunderstood by Luke that he reduces Jesus's power from cosmic Christ to faith-healer? Or is Luke – like all the patriarchs – struggling with the wild feminine – untamable, trouble-making – the lawless one – in Jungian terms, the dark anima?

Luke allows a grudging acceptance of the women with Jesus. They are named, which means they were very important, but they are dismissed as "some women who had been cured of evil spirits and infirmities: Mary, called Magdalene, from whom *seven demons* had gone out, and Joanna, the wife of Herod's steward Chuza, and Susanna." He also mentions "many others, who provided for them out of their resources" who presumably also had been "cured." He had to mention the ones who had the money.

But the ultimate demonstration of sin is Jezebel's perversion of the law in Ahab's name. Ah yes, Jezebel. The Wicked Witch of the West Bank. She's a pagan, a priestess of Baal, and the personification of Evil in the Old Testament. Her demise is apocalyptic – she predicts her own death by wild dogs, which is confirmed in the sentence against Ahab, proclaimed by Elijah (which we don't read in this series in Year C).

Jezebel is a mythical character, but nevertheless is a powerful female presence – otherwise, she never would have been named. In the battle between the Hebrew God and Baal, Jezebel is a major force. She is also the anima – the dark feminine – for Ahab, and perhaps for God as well. When Ahab can't bring himself to really act on his selfish desires, he projects it onto his wife, who acts for him. Have we heard this before? Didn't Adam do the same with Eve? What is it with these patriarchs?

Acting outside the law is not the same as perverting the law, as Paul makes clear, and Jezebel's fate illustrates. If sin (injustice) is indeed a product of the law, then the wild feminine outside the law must be the pure spirit of justice-compassion.

Proper 7
Earth, Wind, and Fire

1 Kings 19:1-15; Isaiah 65:1-9 Psalms 42 and 43; Psalm 22:19-28; Galatians 3:23-29; Luke 8:26-39

In Moses's day, God was known and recognized in the earthquake, the wind, and the fire. We might imagine that Luke's Jesus consigns the demons to the water as the fourth element. It is impossible to know if Luke was making that connection – likely not. But Elijah finds God in the silence. The verse has been translated as "the still small voice" for centuries. But the New RSV translates the verse as "after the fire, a sound of sheer silence." Suppose that rather than an indication of whether there was or was not a new revelation to Elijah, God is indeed found in the silence? Instead of the voice of "conscience,""ego" or "conventional wisdom" – which seems to lead inevitably to the normalcy of civilization and collaboration with Empire – God's will and humanity's creative response are experienced in the silence – just as the universe itself flamed forth from the original depths of darkness and silence: what Starhawk[25] calls the Fifth Sacred Thing – Spirit. "Deep calls to deep," says Psalm 42. "All your waves and your billows have gone over me. By day the Lord commands his steadfast love, and at night his song is with me, a prayer to the God of my life."

Elijah has dedicated his life to restoring God's righteousness to the people. He has succeeded in defeating the powers of the alien god Baal, but still the people do not turn to God, and the King's wife threatens to kill him. Who can blame Elijah for retreating into the wilderness, and complaining to God: "It is enough, now, God. Take away my life. I am no better than my ancestors," who of course created the golden calf while Moses himself was up on the mountain getting the law from God. But God calls Elijah back to that same holy place –

---

[25]Starhawk, author and activist of the Goddess movement and Earth-based, feminist spirituality.
http://www.starhawk.org

Mount Horeb – and out of the silence, Elijah receives an astounding assignment. Elijah must anoint two alien kings to rule over Israel. He must also anoint Elisha to be his successor – perhaps as a reward for being faithful to God, even though he wanted to die under the broom tree. What has happened here? Has God abandoned God's chosen people, Israel? Or is God indeed giving to Elijah a new revelation: expanding the meaning of the promise of Abraham, as Luke's Jesus hints, and as Paul suggests to the Galatians?

In Luke's story, "a man of the city" was possessed by demons. When asked his name, the man replies "Legion" – because, says Luke, there were many demons. When the demons ask Jesus not to send them back to "the abyss," he sends them into a herd of swine instead. Now, swine are unclean animals. So the swineherds must be outcast people – perhaps they are gentiles, even Roman servants. So when the man says his name is "Legion," is he saying his life has been taken over by Roman oppressors? The people of the surrounding country are frightened by Jesus's action in healing/delivering/liberating the man from the oppression of the Roman demons by releasing them into the pigs, who are then destroyed because they run down the bank into the lake and are drowned. The people ask Jesus to leave, and he does. When the liberated man asks to go with him, however, Jesus tells him to go home and let people know "how much God has done for you." But instead of proclaiming how much the Hebrew *God* had done for him, the man proclaims instead how much *Jesus* had done for him.

Perhaps if the man had claimed the Hebrew God instead of the man Jesus, the Romans would not have paid so much attention to Jesus as a threat to Roman authority. Beyond that, however, is the possibility that when Jesus sends the man home, back to his gentile village, he is sending his message of distributive justice-compassion into the heart of the Roman-occupied society.

Suppose the Elijah story does *not* lead directly to Jesus as the culmination of the will of God. Suppose it is a story about the nature of the universe that belongs to God. God is just, and the Earth (the world – the cosmos) belongs to God. We know that whenever one life form falls out of balance with its environment, an adjustment is made. When there is an over-abundance of acorns, the squirrels and deer reproduce to match it – and vice-versa. When there are too many rabbits, predators proliferate until the balance is restored. So if humanity ignores God's righteousness – the natural balance of distributive justice-compassion that is reflected in the fabric of the nature of the cosmos – and if God then acts to restore justice-compassion – why shouldn't God use whatever life form it takes for that restoration?

The point throughout is that salvation means participation in God's realm of distributive justice-compassion, *not* forgiveness for breaking the laws of Moses. Paul's ecstatic message is that the laws of Moses don't matter. What matters is faith that God has restored God's distributive justice-compassion with the death and resurrection of Jesus. Our job is not to conform to the law, but to live in covenant with God.

The orthodox interpretation has been in the context of Jesus's death in payment for petty trespass and saving souls from eternal hell and damnation, not as participants in God's Kingdom of justice-compassion. "Belief" in the promise given to Abraham and passed on through Elijah to Jesus to us has meant belief that Jesus died in substitutionary atonement, not that nothing can separate us from the love of God, as promised to Abraham and his descendants forever. In Isaiah 65, God says, "I will bring forth descendants from Jacob and from Judah inheritors of my mountains; my chosen shall inherit it, and my servants shall settle there." All we have to do is choose to participate. If we choose not to participate, we then are complicit in crimes against divinity, whether we "believe" in Jesus or not.

Paul asks, "does God supply you with the Spirit and work miracles among you by your doing the works of the law, or by your believing what you heard?" The law cannot reconcile us to God's justice-compassion. Only faith in God's covenant can do that. "And if you belong to Christ, then you are Abraham's offspring, heirs according to the promise" says Paul, not heirs according to some rite of passage such as circumcision, or, in later years, through some kind of apostolic succession, or a litmus test in the form of a "confession of faith."

There is no longer, then, Christian or infidel, alien or citizen, enemy or friend, for all are one who participate in God's distributive justice-compassion. Belief that a corpse was resuscitated one early Sabbath morning 2,000 years ago is irrelevant. The heirs of the promise God made to Abraham are the ones who love their enemies.

Proper 8
Yankee Doodle Do or Die

Galatians 5:1, 13-25

President George W. Bush is famously believed to have equated dissent to the war in Iraq with lack of patriotism when he said in a speech that "if you are not with us, you are with the terrorists." Probably the first task when countering an argument is to get the story straight. In the spirit of getting the story straight, the context of that speech was September 20, 2001, and Mr. Bush was referring to other nations in the world, not the American people. But somehow that sentiment – that demand that all nations of the world join the struggle against terrorism – has morphed into a perceived assault on our constitutional right to free speech in opposition to national policy. It isn't true. President Bush never actually accused American citizens of disloyalty for disagreeing with the war in Iraq.

Nevertheless, the perception is out there.

The point here is to illustrate the difference between *patriotism* – which is simply the love of the land of our birth – and *nationalism,* which is a call to arms on behalf of the policies of the government. *Nationalism* appeals to the desire we all have to align ourselves with a cause or an idea that is greater than we perceive ourselves to be. Nationalism arouses the warrior energy, which is most clearly associated with archetypes of masculinity – although women of course, experience those archetypes as well. The warrior energy is the energy of leadership, of protection, of moving outward, of exploration – and of course of defense and conquest. Like all archetypes, the warrior has two sides – a healthy, nurturing, positive side, and a negative, shadow, demonic side. Warrior energy is what inspires us – especially when we are young – to seek out adventure, to explore strange new worlds – to boldly go where no one has gone before. Those strange new worlds might be galaxies, solar systems, planets, ecosystems, and they might be that spark of creativity that propels us outside the ordinary boxes of thought and into new paradigms.

The dark side of the warrior energy is easy to see. Some of the results of the shadow warrior include global warming, Native American reservations, South African apartheid, religious intolerance, and nationalism. The warrior denies himself for the good of the team. The warrior believes what her leaders tell her. Nationalism is therefore dangerous because it arouses that warrior energy, which can be blinded to the truth about what is really going on. Warrior energy desires to apprentice itself to wisdom. But that precious, altruistic, idealistic, desire is betrayed and enslaved by its own demonic shadow when warriors are recruited to a cause and then lied to about the reasons, the methods, the justifications, and the consequences of that cause. Appeals to nationalism only work when there is a political, social, or economic threat to the nation's well-being. September 11, 2001 has been used – brilliantly – to further the cause of nationalism. Worse, that American nationalism has become aligned with – indeed, defined by – fundamentalist Christian religion: a truly terrifying combination because piety then becomes the basic ingredient for judging loyalty. The next thing you know, anyone who is not a fundamentalist Christian is suspect.

The Galatians had apparently accepted the Apostle Paul's story of the meaning of Jesus's death and resurrection – namely, that Jesus's resurrection – his transformation from an earthly presence to a full partnership with God – meant that humankind was also invited to full partnership with God to restore God's distributive justice-compassion to the land. In Paul's interpretation, this partnership with God overturned and made irrelevant the laws of society, most especially Roman law. The Galatians had formed a community based not on Roman law, but on principles that would restore God's realm of justice-compassion to the world: those principles being love, joy, peace, patience, kindness, generosity, faithfulness, gentleness, and self-control. In other words, Covenant, nonviolence, distributive justice, and peace rather than the Roman imperial system of piety, war, and peace through military victory.

Then someone in the early church came along from the opposition to Paul's ideas and insisted that the only way to be a Christian was to obey the Jewish law. So Paul's letter to the

Galatians is an impassioned reading of the riot act regarding the impossibility of living a life of justice-compassion by obeying the law, whether in the first century, or the twenty-first. For example:

In the District of Columbia, there is no safe-haven law that protects from prosecution a woman who abandons her baby on somebody's front doorstep. When a baby is found, the social services workers in the District of Columbia are of course charged with trying to locate the missing mother and reconciling the situation. But if the missing mother is found, she must – by law – be prosecuted for criminal neglect and go to jail and probably lose the child. If she turns herself in, she will be arrested; if she does not turn herself in, she will be arrested. Anyone who assists this woman is also subject to prosecution. Under the law, there is no justice possible.

Perhaps more troubling, under the laws of the State of Maryland, a juvenile who is convicted of a crime is not sent to jail but is sentenced to rehabilitation training for a certain amount of time. A 17-year old boy was convicted of sexually abusing the children he was babysitting. He served his rehab, and apparently successfully completed the program, so the judge sent him home. But the people in his neighborhood did not want him anywhere near his home. The judge said his hands were tied because the juvenile justice system in the State of Maryland is about rehabilitation, not punishment. Paul lays it on the line in Galatians 5 verse 14: "You are called to freedom from the law, because the whole law is summed up in a single commandment: "You shall love your neighbor as yourself." In this example, what is the response that comes from love – justice-compassion?

The most radical statement in Galatians chapter 5 is verse 18: "If you are led by the spirit, you are not subject to the law." In other words, those who follow the way of Jesus will not comply with the machinery that leads to injustice. How can we restore both God's justice-compassion and a political commitment to the classically liberal principles that grounded the Declaration of Independence? In the face of tyrannies of the original King George, Thomas Jefferson insisted: "That all men are created equal. That they are endowed by their creator with certain unalienable rights, that among these are life, liberty, and the pursuit of happiness . . . that whenever any form of Government becomes destructive of these ends, it is the right of the people to alter or to abolish it . . ."

Following is a portion of a litany created by Jim Loney, a member of the Christian Peacemaker Team (CPT) that was captured in Iraq in late 2005 and held for 118 days. CPT is a program of the historic peace churches in the U.S. and Canada, including Brethren, Quaker, and Mennonite churches. Members work on projects in Iraq, Colombia, Palestine, Canada, The Democratic Republic of Congo, and along the U.S.-Mexican border, training people of faith in the principles and practice of nonviolence so that they can enter conflict zones and promote peace.

Jim Loney and the other team members who were with him refused to testify against their captors, and as a result, the people who murdered Tom Fox were not brought to trial. The reasons for not testifying included that their captors would be subject to the death penalty, and that they – like we – were involved in a struggle for survival.

All: With the help of God's grace
One: Let us resist and confront evil everywhere we find it
All: With the help of God's grace
One: With the waging of war
All: We will not comply
One: With the forces of fear
All: We will not comply
One: With laws that betray human life
All: We will not comply
One: With governments that are blind to the sanctity of life
All: We will not comply
One: With economic structures that impoverish and dehumanize
All: We will not comply
One   With the perpetuation of violence
All: We will not comply
One: With the help of God's grace

All: We will struggle for justice, we will stand for what is true, we will love even our enemies, we will resist all evil.

One: Let us abide in God's love

All   Thanks be to God[26]

---

[26]Litany of Resistance – James Loney, Christian Peacemaker Teams (Peace and Justice Support Network, Mennonite Church USA) http://peace.mennolink.org/articles/litofres.html

Proper 9
Elisha's God Trumps Luke's Jesus

2 Kings 5:1-14; Galatians 6:1-16; Luke 10:1-11

These passages have been used for too long to reinforce conventional piety and morality. Where is the radicality of God that is the root of Jesus's teaching? Certainly not in Luke's story of the seventy-two followers who set off on a conversion mission with the order to call down greater destruction than Sodom and Gomorrah on those communities that would not accept their message. According to the Jesus Seminar scholars, by the time Luke's Gospel was written the story "presuppose[d] a context far removed from that of the itinerant Jesus."[27] The only radical idea in Luke's list of instructions to missionaries that reflects Jesus's actual teaching is to "eat whatever is set before you" in violation of the Jewish dietary laws.

The radicality of God may be more clear in the story about the healing of Naaman – the commander of the army of the king of Aram. Faith is not belief about God. Faith is trust in God's word.

Naaman's wife has an Israelite slave who tells about the great prophet who lives in Samaria, who could cure Naaman's leprosy. When the king of Aram learns about this, he agrees to send Naaman immediately with a letter to the king of Israel – presumably so the king of Israel would not think that Naaman was invading with an army. When Naaman arrives at Elisha's house, he is insulted that Elisha does not come out to him, wave his hands over the leprosy, invoke the God of Israel, and *bibbety-bobbety-boo! Alakazam!* the leprosy is gone. Instead, a messenger comes out and tells Naaman to bathe in the Jordan River seven times. Why not bathe in our own river? gripes Naaman. Our rivers are better than the Jordan! And he storms off in a rage. But his servants point out that all he has to do is wash and be clean. So he does. No magic. No ritual. No conventional junk performed by a priest. All that is required is

---

[27]Funk, Hoover, and The Jesus Seminar, *The Five Gospels,* p. 320

trust in the word of God from the representative of Israel's God, the prophet Elisha. What's radical is, you don't have to be Jewish. Gentiles who trust God's word are equally eligible for healing.

Unfortunately, the writer of Luke's story about the seventy-two missionaries had already confused "trust" in God's word with "belief" in Jesus's death and resurrection as atonement for sin. If "trust" in the word of God as received from God's greatest prophet had been the meaning of faith, then even though some communities rejected the word, it would still be said. The word to be trusted was not and is not violent retribution for rejection of God's kingdom. The word to be trusted was and is "peace to this house!" – Covenant, nonviolence, justice-compassion, and peace, whether this message is accepted or not. "Belief" in the death and resurrection of Jesus as atonement for "sin" not only misses the point, it assures that the normalcy of civilization continues to prevail against the radicality of God.

We learned in the readings for Proper 7 that the king of Aram was anointed by God through the prophet Elijah, and whoever escaped from the king of Aram the king of Israel would kill, and whoever escaped from the king of Israel, the prophet Elisha would kill. But God seems to be reaching around the king of Israel and saving Israel's enemies – who keep their word, and follow the instructions of God's prophet. Then even Elisha's servant falls victim to human greed. We aren't supposed to read this part, but it completes the story and the point. Elisha's servant Gehazi succumbs to greed (Paul's "flesh") and pays the price for the corruption that defines the normalcy of civilization. When Elisha declines to accept the gentile Naaman's gifts in exchange for his miraculous healing, Gehazi is scandalized. "As the Lord lives, I will run after him and get something out of him," he says. When he catches up with Naaman, he makes up a story about unexpected company that needs silver and clothing. Naaman not only complies with Elisha's supposed request, he doubles the amount asked for. Shades of Jesus's recommendation found in Matthew 5:40-41: that if the Roman occupier demands your shirt, give him your cloak, or if he demands you carry his bags one mile, go for two.

111

The outsider Naaman is generous to a fault. The insider Gehazi is corrupted and therefore cursed by Elisha with the very same leprosy Naaman was cured of. As Paul writes to the Galatians, "Do not be deceived; God is not mocked, for you reap whatever you sow."

The conventional wisdom throughout is "what goes around comes around." But that's not Jesus's message, and it is certainly not Paul's interpretation. The outsider Naaman trusts the Hebrew God's word and bathes in the River Jordan and is cured. All he had to do was choose to accept Elisha's instruction. At the end of his flaming letter to the Galatians, Paul reiterates the importance of choosing to obey the only law that matters: you shall love your neighbor as yourself. Those who teach otherwise are complying with the prevailing normalcy of civilization, acting in their own self interest, trying in the first century context to fit into the culture and avoid being persecuted – and persecution of the followers of Jesus's way had already begun, as Paul himself knew very well.

Proper 10
Samaritans in the Ditch

Amos 7:7-17; Deuteronomy 30:9-14; Colossians 1:1-14;
Luke 10:25-37; Psalm 82; Psalm 25:1-10

The story of the good Samaritan is probably one of the most loved and most misunderstood parables that Jesus told. Nearly all of us identify with the Samaritan who stops to help a man who had been robbed and left for dead by the side of the road. Hundreds of homeless shelters, feeding programs, and free clinics world-wide may contain the name "Samaritan," but they miss the original point of the parable.[28]

Jesus's contemporaries may have heard him tell the story at a banquet. After the main course has been cleared and the wine and fruit brought out, the political discussions begin, interspersed with jokes and aphorisms about the occupying Romans, godless Greek pagans, Arab traders, and local riff-raff such as the tax collectors, dishonest merchants, and of course, those dirty, shifty-eyed Samaritans, who live in the hills and probably worship the old Canaanite gods and goddesses in contravention of God's law.

Into the raucous profanity Jesus tosses this gem: "Have you heard the one about the man who was going from Jerusalem to Jericho who fell into the hands of robbers? They stripped him and beat him up and left him for dead."

"So what else is new?" the listeners gripe. "The Romans refuse to secure the road. We're all at the mercy of bandits and murderers!"

"Well it just so happens," Jesus goes on, "That a priest was going down that road. When he saw the man, he went out of his way to avoid him. In the same way, a Levite came to the place, took one look at him, and crossed the road to avoid him."

"Probably thought he was dead. Unclean. Can't touch him. It's the law."

"But this Samaritan who was traveling that way came to where he was and —"

---

[28]Ibid., 324.

"Hah! Picked what was left of his pockets, right?"

"– was moved to pity at the sight of him."

Jesus has everyone's full attention at this point, and escalates the preposterousness of the scene with every following phrase: "He went up to him and bandaged his wounds –"

["huh?"]

"– poured olive oil and wine on them. Then he hoisted him up *on his own animal*, brought him to an inn, and looked after him."

"Get out!"

"The *next day*, he took out two silver coins, which he gave to the innkeeper, and said, 'Look after him, and on my way back, I'll reimburse you for any extra expense you have had.'"

The entire room falls out laughing.

It would be fun to remain a fly on the wall at this point and listen to the discussion among people who identified *not* with the rescuer, but with the victim. The question was not to whom am I a neighbor, as Luke casts the story with his preceding dialogue about the law of love, but from whom can I expect help? Clearly, Jesus's audience would never expect assistance from an enemy like a Samaritan. It would be like accepting donations from Hamas to the fund for 9/11 victims.

But what about the traditional interpretation of this parable? Who are the priests and the Levites of this day that are caught up in the power of sin, to use authentic Pauline language? The Letter to the Colossians was likely not written by Paul. Paul speaks of sin as an enslaving power, not a petty trespass or misdeed. Nevertheless, this writer says "[God] has rescued us from the power of darkness and transferred us into the kingdom of [God's] beloved Son." Just because we are presented with these readings, doesn't mean we can't use the authentic Paul's interpretation.

When we superimpose the metaphor of sin as an entrapping or enslaving "power of darkness" over the traditional reading of the parable, the priest and the Levite in today's terms might represent institutions such as a state-run medical emergency program and a health insurance company. Clearly our victim cannot expect to receive help from either one, especially if he's not a legal citizen of the United States, and even if he were, his health insurance company would deny coverage because the treatment was not pre-approved.

Middle class Americans lose whether we interpret this parable in the traditional way, or from the point of view of the victim. We are so caught up in the "power of darkness" – meaning the day-to-day minutiae of surviving as individuals, families, neighborhoods, social networks – that we have no time to pay attention to the people tossed into the margins. And when we are tossed into the margins ourselves, the very institutions we thought we had created to help us – such as the Food & Drug Administration, FEMA, the U.S. Congress – fail us.

How much longer can we pass by on the other side? In Psalm 82, God says to the high council of Gods in the Universe, "How long will you judge unjustly and show partiality to the wicked? Give justice to the weak and the orphan; maintain the right of the lowly and the destitute. Rescue the weak and the needy; deliver them from the hand of the wicked."

Amos was "a herdsman, and a dresser of sycamore trees" when God chose him to prophesy to the people of Israel, trying to restore God's justice-compassion to the land in opposition to King Jeroboam's retributive imperial rule. But the priest of Bethel (Amaziah) tells Amos to go prophesy to the land of Judah, not Israel, because Bethel is the King's sanctuary and a temple of the kingdom. In other words, King Jeroboam is a good guy, a God-Worshiper, a man of faith. Amaziah has sold out to Empire. He tells Amos to cross to the other side of the Bethel road; King Jeroboam is his own justice. But Amos says to the priest, if you don't listen to the word of the Lord God of Israel, your family will be destroyed, and your people will go into exile.

We are the gods in the universe, who have neither knowledge nor understanding. When the gods walk around in darkness, then all the foundations of the earth are shaken. What are the foundations of the earth? God's distributive justice-compassion. Without distributive justice, whether it is economic justice, social justice, political justice, or ecological justice, the normalcy of civilization trumps God's radicality, and everything perishes. Mountaintops are removed for strip-mining; oceans are over-fished; rain forests are bulldozed; climate changes.

Perhaps it is appropriate after all to name our faith-based social service programs "Samaritan." We are our own worst enemy. That's us in the ditch.

Proper 11
Mary, Martha, and Zen

Amos 8:1-12; Genesis 18:1-10; Psalm 52; Psalm 15;
Colossians 1:15-28; Luke 10:38-42

Because Luke probably made this story up out of whole cloth, we can do with it whatever we wish. Jesus never had this encounter, never hinted that women disciples are better (or worse) than women servant supporters of his ministry. This is not about women's liberation. It's about choosing to follow Jesus's Way into God's Kingdom. In Rev. Dr. Matthew Fox's interpretation,[29] it's about the Zen of following Jesus's Way and doing the great work of God's Kingdom of justice-compassion. "Zen" as in letting go and letting be. Let go of the mind chatter *about* being a disciple, activist, whatever, and just do it.

In Matthew Fox's theology of original blessing and the Four Paths of Creation Spirituality, "birth is the logical outcome of those who follow the path of letting go and letting be." Fox calls that process of letting go the *via negativa* – the spiritual state of nothingness, from which all new thought flares forth (*via creativa*), whether it is a new theory of physics, a postmodern multi-media techno-cosmic mass, or quilting. Creative thought allows the birth of creative work, which supports what Fox calls the "great work" of justice-compassion – Fox's *via transformativa*.

The combination of readings for Proper 11 offers the same metaphors of fruitfulness and spiritual maturity that Meister Eckhart used in the fourteenth century, and then Matthew Fox used in his twentieth century commentary to enlighten theology and cosmology over a span of 600 years. Amos talks about the basket of summer fruit that will become famine because the people turn away from God's great work of justice-compassion. Sarah and Abraham – in their spiritual maturity and trust in God's word – will bear the fruit of a son, and be the ancestors of many nations. Psalm 52 warns that evil doers will not succeed; Psalm 15 says that those who will dwell on God's holy

---

[29]See Fox, *Breakthrough*, Sermons 20 and 34.

hill will be "those who walk blamelessly, and do what is right." The only piece that is a clanging gong in the ensemble is the Colossians rant about "Christ" being "the head of the body the church," and the theology of substitutionary atonement, which the real Paul had no time for. Perhaps it's a way out for orthodox preachers who don't want to consider unconventional interpretations of Luke's Mary/Martha drama about sibling rivalry and woman's real place in the home.

Meister Eckhart's Sermon 20 talks about how "Martha" represents the mature person – the "wife" who bears fruit, who serves the master. Mary in Luke's story is the young sycophant, enamored of the guru, unconscious, and trapped in ego-involvement. Mary Magdalene's aria, "I don't know how to love him," from *Jesus Christ Superstar* comes to mind. But gender is irrelevant to this discussion. "Wife" and "virgin" are metaphors for Eckhart. Martha has let go even of letting go, in Fox's interpretation. "[Eckhart] observes that what forces people to remain virgins and not move on to bearing fruit is that you will have no trust in either God or yourself until you have accomplished the deed you have taken up with egotistical attachment. In other words, what makes us compulsive grabbers who are unable to let go and let be is lack of trust and confidence. This confidence is not merely a matter of faith in God but also of faith in ourselves."[30] Old Sarah probably was laughing for good reason on a number of levels, not to mention the age of Abraham.

Eckhart imagines that Martha's complaint that Mary isn't helping is really a bit of gentle ribbing to get Mary to let go and let be – to get out of her mind and into the fruitfulness of service (wife). For Eckhart, it's not about contemplation being better than action, or ideas being more valuable than "work," or an allegory about women's role in the early church.

In Sermon 34, Eckhart continues with the metaphor of a spiritually mature person (Martha) living in depth with God, not enamored with the idea of being a disciple. Mary's "better part" is that she is learning to live and work, but is not there yet. Fox: "Only later was Mary so full of the Holy Spirit that she knew

---

[30]Fox, *Breakthrough*, 285.

what true service meant. She learned how to work and to do works of compassion. . . . The full expression of the Spirit then, is in our work that brings about the Spirit's intentions."[31]

The trick is to know the difference between the fruits of Empire and the fruits of the Spirit.

---

[31]*Ibid.*, 489

Proper 12
Resurrected into Presence

Hosea 1:2-10; Genesis 18:20-32; Psalm 85; Colossians 2:6-19;
Luke 11:1-13

Orthodoxy can have a field day with these readings. In Hosea, God disowns Israel as a whore; in Genesis, Abraham bargains with God to save Sodom for the sake of ten righteous people; and the writer of Colossians warns against being misled by "human tradition" and "the elemental spirits of the universe." Improper sinners, listen up! Your only hope is that your "father" in "heaven" forgives your "trespasses" without "leading you into temptation," says that collaborator Luke. But thanks be to God, writes pseudo-Paul, "when you were buried with [Christ] in baptism, you were also raised with [Christ] through faith in the power of God who raised [Christ] from the dead."

Who can make sense of any of this in a postmodern world? We might do better to find a good quote from Rumi or Maya Angelou for this Sunday.

> *Rumi*: "I called through your door, 'The mystics are gathering in the street. Come out!' 'Leave me alone. I'm sick.' 'I don't care if you're dead!' Jesus is here, and he wants to resurrect somebody!"[32]

> *Maya Angelou*: "You, created only a little lower than the angels, have crouched too long in the bruising darkness, have lain too long facedown in ignorance, your mouths spilling words armed for slaughter. The Rock cries out to us today, You may stand upon me; but do not hide your face."[33]

Luke and the Elves want to force the lectionary readings into demonstrating how God answers the prayers of the righteous. But Jesus actually talked about three very different conditions or ideas: God's imperial rule (God's kingdom of distributive justice-compassion); hospitality; and trust. In the

---

[32]Barks, *The Essential Rumi*, 201.

[33]Angelou, *On the Pulse of Morning*.

"Jesus prayer," Jesus is likely to have said only the first two lines: "Abba-Father, may your name be revered. Impose your imperial rule – [in opposition to Rome's]." Luke's Jesus probably did tell the story about the friend demanding assistance in the middle of the night, but it's about hospitality, not how God answers persistent prayer. In *The Five Gospels,* the translation has Luke's Jesus say, "I tell you, even though you won't get up and give the friend anything out of friendship, yet you will get up and give the other whatever is needed because you'd be ashamed not to." God's answer to persistent prayer has nothing to do with it. The point that Luke misses is people acting with distributive justice-compassion and out of the essential hospitality that assured that life could be lived in such stark times. Luke's Jesus probably did also tell his followers "Rest assured: everyone who asks receives, everyone who seeks finds, and for the one who knocks it is opened." But again it's not about petitionary prayer to an interventionist God. It's about trust in living out the ongoing work of restoring God's distributive justice-compassion. Jesus likely said it to reassure those who went out as he did into itinerant ministry.

Pseudo Paul also misses the point of the authentic Paul when he writes about baptism as burial. In Romans 6:3-5, authentic Paul is making the point that baptism is the symbol that those who choose to participate in the ongoing work of restoring God's distributive justice-compassion are "dead" to the Empire, and dead to the temptations of the normalcy of civilization. Pseudo Paul has literalized the metaphor and as a result has contributed to the heresies of the human tradition he rails against that have culminated in twenty-first century Empire, corporate greed, and the ravages of global warming – or in the words of John Dominic Crossan, "American Christian fundamentalism's divine ethnic cleansing and transcendental cosmicide."[34]

The writer of Colossians has a point: "See to it that no one takes you captive through philosophy and empty deceit. . . ." Orthodoxy and tradition have rendered us dead to the natural world and trapped in the illusion of past and future. We are

---

[34]Crossan, *God and Empire,* 200.

indeed sick, and want only to be left alone in our unconsciousness. So long as we are stuck in the triumphs or the tragedies of the past, we either anticipate or dread the future, and entirely squander the opportunities and responsibilities of the present moment. The Jesus prayer asks only for the bread we need "day by day," not tomorrow and tomorrow and tomorrow. A better reading to pair with Luke's Jesus prayer might be Exodus 16. The bread that fell from heaven on the Israelites in the wilderness only lasted for one day – except for the double portion provided on the Sabbath. Anyone who tried to hoard it found that "it bred worms and became foul."

Jesus is here to resurrect us into presence, to remind us to trust the process we have signed onto – if we have indeed signed on. Only then are we invited to stand on the Rock.

Proper 13
Call it Karma

Hosea 11:1-11; Ecclesiastes 1:2, 12-14; 2:18-23;
Colossians 3:1-11; Luke 12:13-21

Clergy friends warn about trying to tie together all of the readings for any particular Sunday as futile, if not vanity. But searching for a thread makes sense. If there were no thread, then the RCL would seem to be some kind of mathematically determined repertoire, which occasionally accidentally synchronizes. In this group, the reading that really does not track with the others is Colossians. The Elves have cherry-picked yet another diatribe against "whatever is earthly: fornication, impurity, passion, evil desire, and greed (which is idolatry)" then claim in the face of the reading from Hosea that "God is coming on those who are disobedient." Hosea's God can't bring himself to punish his people, even though they "are bent on turning away from me." Luke's Jesus is made to miss his own joke and piously say that those who store up treasures for themselves but are not rich toward God will somehow be brought to an early death, just as they are congratulating themselves on their good fortune. Meanwhile, the Preacher who wrote Ecclesiastes in the name of the great King Solomon says it's all useless anyway, and wisdom means nothing if after all your years of hard work you leave it to some idiot at the end.

Before we abandon all this as hopeless irrelevancy, let's separate these readings from the orthodox idea that the Old Testament finds its fulfillment in the New Testament. Then let's assume that the scholars of the Jesus Seminar are onto something, and that Jesus was a traveling sage and teacher of the Wisdom tradition in first century Palestine. Let's also assume that a lot of that wisdom Jesus taught had as its purpose the undermining of the Roman occupation that was indeed wooing some people away from the Jewish concern with God's distributive justice-compassion; and let's take the version of the parable of the rich fool not from Luke and his editorializing, but from the sayings gospel of Thomas 63:1-3.

So Jesus is relaxing around a fire with his followers after a meal on the road. The wine is passing hand to hand, and some of the women are also participating, because on this particular occasion there are no "pharisees" or "tax collectors" or other collaborators with Rome around who might object. Perhaps they are discussing the unfairness of those monied classes who can buy their way out of just about anything, including God's law. Maybe, because Jesus was a teacher of the Wisdom tradition, they knew what King Solomon had to say about the futility of working all your life and then giving it over to someone who either won't know how to manage it so that it can stay in the family, or – as is more likely, given the presumed poverty of Jesus's itinerant band – why bother working all your life and then losing it all to debt? Things may have been getting a bit gloomy there around the fire, especially since an entire family may have just joined them who had indeed lost everything, and just barely escaped selling themselves into slavery.

Jesus says, "There was a rich person who had a great deal of money."

The group collectively roll their eyes and poke each other. "Here it comes."

"So this rich person says, 'I shall invest my money so that I may sow, reap, plant, and fill my storehouses with produce, so that I may lack nothing.'"

"I know that's right!"

"These were the things he was thinking in his heart," Jesus continues, "but that very night he died."

Silence. Then one of the women lets loose with a long giggle, and they are all rolling and laughing and slapping each other. Even the new family can join in the joke, because for now – and Jesus is always insisting that "now" is all there is – they have bread and wine and a place to stay. Living well is the best revenge.

The lectionary usually coincides with the agricultural cycle of the seasons in the northern hemisphere. Luke's version of Jesus's joke sets the story at harvest time. North of the equator, August 1-2 marks the Celtic cross-quarter day of Lughnasad – called Lammas or "Loaf Mass" in the medieval Celtic Christian tradition. It is the season of the first harvest. The bread for communion at this first harvest time was made from the first of the grains of the year. Recent years in the U.S. have seen drought plague much of the country that usually supplies fruits, vegetables, and grains. At the same time, because of misguided ideas about using a food substance (corn) to feed our gluttonous automobiles, many of the unprofitable orchards and other pieces of acreage that people may own ,which were earlier cleared for hay sales, have been planted in corn. Corn prices are soaring, and so are corn futures. The desperate and the profiteers alike are throwing all their eggs into the ethanol basket.

What's wrong with this picture? Jesus reminds us that as the Preacher says, it's all blowing in the wind anyway. Qoheleth[35] (the "Preacher") makes two points about "the good." The first is that everyone's duty is to love God and keep God's commandments. Jesus constantly reminds us that that is what it means to participate in God's realm of distributive justice-compassion. The second point the Preacher makes is that life is God's gift, and life is the portion of God's realm for which humanity is responsible.

Jaded existentialists might agree with the portion of Ecclesiastes that the Elves have selected, and with macabre humor point out that "life is hell, then you die." Twenty-first century postmodern minds have moved beyond Jesus's joke about the rich man. Kenneth Lay (the deposed CEO of Enron) went to his grave convinced that he had done nothing wrong. The fact that he was sentenced to a long prison term just was so incomprehensible to him that he literally died of a broken heart. This is not a joke. This is at least a tragedy, but more than that, it is dangerous to be so caught up in a paradigm that we can't see any alternative. Regardless of which paradigm we swim in, like the fish who has no clue where the hooked worm comes from, we can be destroyed by our unconsciousness. Choosing to live in God's realm of distributive justice-compassion does not mean that we blithely ignore the realities of the normalcy of civilization and the seductions of Empire. By the same token, to consciously or unconsciously sell out to Empire and immediate

---

[35]National Council of Churches, *The Harper Collins Study Bible*, 987-988.

self-interest, to act in ways that do not sustain life – human and non-human – is the height of irresponsibility. To the extent that we ignore the consequences of unsustainable policies, whether economic or political, collective or individual, we indeed court the "wrath of God," not as apocalyptic interventionist retribution, but simply as the result.

Call it Karma.

Proper 14
Belief Cannot Be Trusted

Isaiah 1:1, 10-20; Genesis 15:1-6; Hebrews 11:1-3, 8-16;
Luke 12:32-40

The Christian Science Monitor of Friday, August 3, 2007 featured a front-page sidebar story under the heading "Turkish Export. Islamic creationist group launches glitzy, global blitz." If ever there were a wake-up call regarding the chasm between premodern belief systems and postmodern rationalism, this is it.

The Foundation for Scientific Research, an Islamic creationist group, has become a household name in Istanbul. The group says it is distributing its books in fifty-nine languages world-wide. Turkey is now the headquarters of creationism in the Islamic world. The Foundation's "Atlas" is available through Amazon.com's special virtual bookstore, and in Islamic bookshops everywhere. The founder of the Foundation for Scientific Research is Adnan Oktar, who sees most of the world's problems as stemming from Darwin's theory of evolution. The *Monitor*'s Yigal Schleifer wrote, "Unlike fundamentalist Christian creationists, Oktar does not claim the earth was created only a few thousand years ago. Instead, he argues that fossils show that creatures from millions of years ago looked just like the creatures of today, thus disproving evolution. . . . [T]he success of the . . . books, at least in the Islamic world, can be attributed to a need for harmonizing modern life with traditional Islamic beliefs."

When Copernicus proved scientifically that the earth travels around the sun, the Church in its panic to retain its credibility and its political power had to prove that its teachings were also scientifically based. *Mythos* quickly morphed into *logos.* In other words, metaphor became literalized so that church leaders would not look like idiots. Needless to say, much of the metaphor that shrouded the figure of the historical Jesus coalesced into such implausible fact as the virgin birth, the revival of a corpse dead for three days, and the bodily ascension of the risen Jesus in the general direction of Antares.

Myth gives meaning to the mysteries of life, and myth is always profoundly true. But myth cannot be made into fact. Truth *believed* is a lie.

What does this have to do with the RCL readings for Proper 14? Consider the traditional orthodox theology reflected in Genesis, Luke, and Hebrews. Faith is belief in the covenant of Abraham (Gen. 15:1-6); faith is belief that Jesus will come again in judgment (Luke 12:35-40); faith is belief that Christians are strangers in a strange land, and that God has prepared a City in heaven for them (Hebrews 11:1-3, 8-16).

A note in the RCL explains that one set of readings pairs the Old Testament with the Gospel. The other set of readings provides alternatives that are more-or-less consecutive in the Old Testament, and not associated with the New Testament. This may explain why the lectionary seems at times to be put together by drunken elves. The authors go on: "For all these Sundays between Pentecost and Advent, churches and denominations may determine which of these patterns better serves their needs. Some denominations will accept one or both patterns for all their congregations; others may choose to let local liturgy planners determine which of these two patterns better serves their needs. The Revised Common Lectionary does not propose one set as more favored than the other, *but the use of the two patterns should not be mixed.*" (Emphasis mine.)

Without mixing the readings, there is often no counter to the prevailing orthodoxy. The scriptures relied upon by Christians for 2,000 years must be reclaimed to the extent possible in the light of present-day cosmology and the physical realities faced by all beings on Planet Earth. Before we throw the Christian baby out with the scriptural bathwater, let's beg to differ with the tradition.

Clark N. Ross, of Northbrook, Illinois wrote in a letter to the editor of the *Christian Century* reflecting on the 2007 massacre of students at Virginia Tech University, "What a shame that in all the centuries since Jesus uttered similar words, we of the Christian tradition have failed to accept the obvious answer: the God you have in mind doesn't exist. This loving, all-powerful father-God we inherited from our Jewish forebears is an illusion. If God is anything at all, such a reality is whatever love, truth, justice, and beauty you and I are able to manifest and to share."[36]

Faith in the context of a postmodern cosmology means trust in a *kenotic* "god" that cannot exist in the absence of justice-compassion. That *kenotic* "god" can only exist where justice-compassion is allowed to flourish. Myth provides the meaning that underlies trust in the cosmic matrix that contains all life forms. For postmodern minds, trapped in premodern belief systems, the myth has to be reclaimed from judgment to liberation – from condemnation for disobedience toward a projection of our own powerlessness to salvation through participation in the *kenotic* realm of distributive justice-compassion, which thunders from the pen of the writer of Isaiah:

> Hear the word of the Lord, you rulers of Sodom! Listen to the teachings of our God, you people of Gomorrah! What to me is the multitude of your sacrifices, says the Lord; . . . when you come to appear before me, who asked this from your hand? Trample my courts no more; bringing offerings is futile; incense is an abomination to me. New moon and sabbath and calling of convocation – I cannot endure solemn assemblies with iniquity . . . When you stretch out your hands, I will hide my eyes from you; even though you make many prayers, I will not listen; your hands are full of blood. Wash yourselves; make yourselves clean; . . . cease to do evil, learn to do good; seek justice, rescue the oppressed, defend the orphan, plead for the widow. . . . If you are willing and obedient, you shall eat the good of the land; but if you refuse and rebel, you shall be devoured by the sword; for the mouth of the Lord has spoken."

Schleifer ends his article by pointing out that "[w]hen Science magazine conducted a survey of thirty-four countries last August, Turkey had the *second-lowest acceptance* rate of

---

[36]Letter to the editor, *The Christian Century*, August 7, 2007.

129

the theory of evolution (*the United States had the lowest.*)"
(Emphasis added.) It is vitally important to get a handle on what
it is that creationists believe, not in order to deconstruct it or
refute it, but to work from a grounding in justice-compassion to
counter the terror that controls the lives of people who *believe*,
but cannot *trust* what Hebrews calls "the assurance of things
hoped for, the conviction of things not seen."

Proper 15
Guardian of the Fire

Isaiah 5:1-7; Psalm 80:1-19; Psalm 82; Hebrews 11:29-12:2;
Luke 12:49-56; Thomas 10

The "cloud of witnesses" is a litany of the Judeo-Christian journey, and the promise of the power of the Christ coming again. This portion of the sermon by the writer of Hebrews has been used by would-be preachers and genuine prophets of Christianity for nearly two millennia. In his last speech, Dr. Martin Luther King Jr. made reference to those who did not receive what was promised in their lifetimes, but who, like Moses and King himself, had been to the mountain top and had been privileged to see the promised land. King was talking about a vision of human justice. Too often the metaphor devolves into threats of hell-fire and damnation. Isaiah's "wild grapes" must be rooted out and destroyed. The writer of Psalm 80 begs God not to abandon the vine that God brought out of Egyptian bondage. Writings become scripture when the metaphor that is used awakens an archetypal response to a specific spiritual condition. The archetypal words continue to resonate and so the writing is reinterpreted long after the original reason for creating the metaphor has been forgotten. The readings do indeed "interpret the present time" in which they were written. The trick is knowing how (and whether) to interpret them now.

Luke's interpretation of what Jesus was reported to have said no longer serves postmodern spiritual realities (and perhaps post-Christian, if by post-Christian we mean post-orthodoxy). Indeed, the scholars of The Jesus Seminar agreed that Luke's Jesus probably never expressed the wish that he had already set the earth ablaze (presumably to cleanse it of sin), nor did he claim that he had come to bring conflict.

Because these commentaries take the position that Jesus's message was nonviolent and radically inclusive, Luke's interpretation can be jettisoned – except for the jibe: "You phonies! You know the lay of the land and can read the face of the sky, so why don't you know how to interpret the present

131

time?" The "present time" for Luke was a time of persecution of Christian communities who were unwilling to collaborate with Roman social and political norms. The "present time" for the twenty-first century presents no less of an apocalypse for humanity, not because of personal trespass, but because the normalcy of civilization has resulted in the political and social pollution of the earth, the air, the fire, the water. We misinterpret the times to our own peril. The judgment of an interventionist god has nothing to do with it.

Once again, let's defy the demand of the creators of the RCL and incorporate the alternative reading of Psalm 82 into the discussion. Psalm 82 describes a dramatic council of the gods of all nations, presided over by the God of Israel. He rises and accuses them of ignoring their mandate to ensure justice for the weak and poor. The gods have neglected their duty to the extent that "the foundations of the earth are shaken." As a result, God demotes the other gods to the status of human beings, to die like mortals, and "fall like any prince" because injustice violates the integrity of the universe.

This takes us far beyond the scope of the Church's concern with petty trespass and dogmatic heresies, or fundamentalism's obsession with purity and retributive terror. Like the gods who walked in the darkness with neither knowledge nor understanding, twenty-first century Western civilization has ignored the consequences of commercial exploitation and ecological, social, and political injustice. Eastern civilizations are showing signs of following the same ruinous course, as evidenced by China's Three Gorges Dam, the refusal by other Southeast Asian governments to cooperate with the World Health Organization in disease prevention, and the disastrous short-cuts taken by Eastern manufacturers of goods for trade with the West.

Perhaps the God of Israel demoted the gods of other nations because as gods, they had no excuse. Their walk in the darkness must have been a deliberate choice. Certainly it is a deliberate choice on the part of the United States Congress and the current president to subsidize non-renewable sources of energy; to cut taxes to the extent that our bridges are falling into our rivers; to support short-term economic gain against long-term solutions; to incorporate into the foreign policy of the most powerful economy on the Planet the heresy of Christian Zionist apocalypticism.

The sayings Gospel of Thomas quotes Jesus in a quite different way, and without Luke's pious context for the edification of the early Christian community. In Thomas, Jesus's unedited words are not about redemption: "I have cast fire upon the world, and look, I'm guarding it until it blazes." The phrase takes the imagination like the grass fire it evokes. What fire has Jesus cast upon the world if not the fire of trust in God's realm of distributive justice-compassion? What fire has Jesus cast upon the world if not the fire of passionate commitment to the ongoing Great Work? What fire has Jesus cast upon the world if not the fire of the radicality of God, which only needs a breath *(ruah)* to flare forth into an inferno of deliverance from injustice? Jesus is the Guardian of the Watchtower of the South and the element of fire – to use Western esoteric metaphor – the quickening fire that cleanses, heals, purifies, and drives the passion of our hearts.

Proper 16
Blood of Abel, Blood of Jesus

Jeremiah 1:4-10; Psalm 71:1-6; Isaiah 58:9b-14;
Hebrews 12:18-30; Psalm 103:1-8; Luke 13:10-17

Fortunately the RCL for Proper 16 gives an "out" to preachers whose eyes glaze over at the prospect of plowing through the metaphor in the Hebrews passage. Besides, orthodox theology has been there and done that *ad nauseam*. The sermon writer's point actually starts with a portion that got left out, namely Hebrews 12:14-17: an admonition to "See to it that no one fails to obtain the grace of God; that no root of bitterness springs up and causes trouble. See to it that no one becomes like Esau, an immoral and godless person who sold his birthright for a single meal. . . ." Then he invokes Moses on Mount Sinai, the fire and smoke, and the apocalypse to come, ending with the self-righteous claim that *we* are "receiving a kingdom that cannot be shaken" because *we* do *acceptable* worship, because our God will burn us up in hell if we don't.

Ho hum.

A "Bible-thumping liberal" might stick with the call of Jeremiah to prophetic service, and Psalm 71, a prayer for life-long protection. Then throw in Luke's fabrication about the woman who was bent in two (probably by an aggressive version of osteoarthritis), and healed by Jesus on the Sabbath (gasp!), in defiance of those nasty leaders of the local church who think that obeying the law is more important than justice. That sermon practically writes itself. But it's much more challenging to start by tossing Luke's story into the circular file. The Jesus Seminar scholars find no parallels in the other Gospels. Luke is his own source on this one. That leaves us with Isaiah 58:9b-14, Psalm 103:1-8, and Hebrews 12:18-30 (or to be fair, 14-30).

The writer of Hebrews reminds his readers or listeners that God and God's realm are not something that can be perceived with any of the physical senses. Instead, he says, we are part of the spiritual realm, and are members of the spiritual assembly of the righteous. We have come to Jesus, "the mediator of a new covenant that speaks a better word than the blood of Abel."

This is powerful metaphor that calls the people of the early Christian Way into a living realm.

That realm for the writer of Hebrews is a realm of apocalyptic judgment: "Yet once more I will shake not only the earth but also the heaven" the writer's God says. Then the writer explains (again in apocalyptic language) that God's phrase "yet once more" means "the removal of what is shaken – that is created things – so that what cannot be shaken may remain."

Even though the Hebrews passage points to a transcendent god, it is still an anthropomorphic projection – a theistic visualization. Further, the transcendent god "warns" about a final judgment from an overarching firmament in a triple-decker universe. Postmodern minds that are not stuck in the suspension of disbelief that is required of most church goers are just as uncomfortable with premodern cosmology as we are with literal theism. Still, the ancient metaphor resonates. "You have not come to something that can be touched . . . we are receiving a kingdom that cannot be shaken . . . we offer to God . . . reverence and awe; for indeed our God is a consuming fire."

Suppose we press the preacher to step into another level – using the same metaphor, but moving from a transcendent interventionist deity to an imminent panentheistic spirit; from a heavenly kingdom of retributive justice after death to a seamless realm here and now, with no veil between the worlds, where distributive justice-compassion reigns?

The Elves seem to have cherry-picked the passages from Isaiah in order to support the orthodox piety reflected in the usual interpretation granted to the writer of Hebrews. "If you remove the yoke from among you, the pointing of the finger, the speaking of evil . . . then your light shall rise in the darkness and your gloom be like the noonday" (58:9ff). But the entire chapter 58 is calling for a much deeper response, as Isaiah points out the difference between false and true worship: Look, you serve your own interest on your fast day, Isaiah accuses. "Look, you fast only to quarrel and fight . . . Such fasting as you do today will not make your voice heard on high. . . . Is not this the fast that I choose: to loose the bonds of injustice, to undo the thongs of the yoke, to let the oppressed go free . . to share your bread with the hungry, and bring the homeless poor into your house . . . Then your light shall break forth like the dawn, and your healing will spring up quickly."

The writer of Hebrews tells us that acceptable worship is to give thanks, with reverence and awe. Such a response does not come from the intellect or the egoistic mind, but only from the soul – from the stillness deep within. The Creation Spirituality tradition articulated by Matthew Fox suggests that awe and wonder are the first emotions that arise in the presence of the cosmos (*via positiva*.) From that ecstatic height, we normally quickly descend into a realization of our own inadequacy or imperfection *(via negativa)*. Most of us do not ultimately bottom out in the void of despair. Some spark of divinity – God's consuming fire – ignites our own creativity, and we respond with the Psalmist, "Bless the Lord O my soul, and bless God's holy name; who redeems your life from the grave . . . and crowns you with love and compassion."

Even though the language is apocalyptic, the reading from Hebrews completes the metaphor of the promised land as the kingdom that cannot be shaken. We are reminded that while God was a pillar of fire by night, guarding the people as they rested on their journey, God was also "a devouring fire, a jealous God," who does not look kindly upon those who forget or ignore the covenant (Deuteronomy 4:24). Some of us – like Esau, in the portion of Hebrews we're not supposed to consider in Year C – break the covenant and sell our birthright – our rightful place in the cosmos, our true home in the realm of justice-compassion – in exchange for our immediate self-interest – Esau's "mess of pottage."

To sell our birthright is a crime against divinity. O.J. Simpson's recent book taunts even the world of retributive justice: "If I Did It" begs the question, "what can you do about it?" NFL star Michael Vic copped a plea that made the legal consequences of his actions a right of passage into a travesty of "manhood." Vic and O.J. may yet truly repent. But the odds of their doing so are not good, given the track record begun by Esau in the ongoing course of the normalcy of civilization. From the point of view of the sermon in Hebrews, they may find no chance, "even though [they seek] the blessing with tears." We shall see.

The "blood of Abel" cries out for retributive justice. The new Covenant mediated by the blood of Jesus means abandonment of self-interest for distributive justice-compassion.

Proper 17
Sacrifices Pleasing to God

Jeremiah 2:4-13; Psalm 81:1, 10-16; Sirach 10:12-18;
Proverbs 25:6-7; Psalm 112; Luke 14:1, 7-14;
Hebrews 13:1-8, 15-16

Sirach, Proverbs, and Luke are all about convention. Psalm 112 is about justice-compassion (righteousness), but conveniently supports the attitude expressed by the other readings if "righteousness" means "morally right, virtuous, law-abiding" (*Oxford Dictionary and Thesaurus, American Edition*, 1996). Pride, says ben Sirach, begins with forsaking the Lord. But this pride is about humiliation and exaltation among nations, not the kind of personal, individual, egotistical behavior illustrated in the Proverbs passage, where we are advised not to push ahead of our station, because it is better to be invited up to the head table than to be asked to move down next to the kitchen. Luke happily refers to this meaning in his lengthy discussion about proper behavior at a wedding feast. It is Luke's topic, not Jesus's. Jesus would have known all about the Wisdom teachings. Nothing new here. Besides, both Luke and ben Sirach are talking about the piety of Empire, not the radical inclusiveness of the Kingdom of God.

Luke's favorite topics for discussion at banquets are the appropriateness of healing on the Sabbath, and "concern" for the poor. He is telling the first century Christian community not to participate in the Roman custom of patronage – where a patron would give a feast for a client, thereby obligating the client to repay in kind in order to keep the social system functioning. The social patronage system controlled every aspect of Roman society, "from gods to emperors, emperors to countries, aristocrats to cities, and . . . from any have to any have not . . . structur[ing] all of society at every level . . . [n]eeded by rulers, praised by philosophers, proclaimed by inscriptions, and used by everyone."[37] Patronage was a hierarchical, vertical, social system, and everyone, from slave to

---

[37]Crossan and Reed, *In Search of Paul*, 297.

emperor, was a client to a patron above him or her, and was in turn a patron to the next one below. The emperor ultimately was client to the gods.

Luke has his Jesus say to invite the outcasts, who are unable to repay. While this seems disingenuous to twenty-first century minds, the Empire is very happy to hear this message coming from the Christian community. If the disenfranchised are fed, they won't foment rebellion against the injustices of daily life. "Concern" for the poor by the twenty-first century church means that taxes that might get earmarked for social safety net programs can instead be diverted into what really matters to Empire: war, and victory – peace through hegemony – not distributive justice.

In the cherry-picked portions of the Hebrews sermon, the Elves would have us concentrate on "Jesus Christ . . . the same yesterday and today and forever, . . . and through him let us offer a sacrifice of praise to God, that is the fruit of lips that confess his name. Do not neglect to do good and to share what you have, for such sacrifices are pleasing to God." If the Hebrews sermon was indeed written between the years 60 and 95 of the first century, then the writer would still have been influenced by the Roman Empire, and because it was based on the Greek Septuagint, the scriptures would have been interpreted in the light of belief in Jesus. But what was that belief? The core of the "belief" seems to have been eliminated from the reading, reducing it to yet another pious admonition about morality: "Let the marriage bed be undefiled. . . . Keep your lives free from the love of money . . ."

If we read the portion between verses 8 and 16, we find that the preacher cautions us not to be carried away "by all kinds of strange teachings," for the heart is "strengthened by grace," not regulated by arbitrary rules. We need to be careful here because these same verses can be construed as antisemitic. Perhaps that is why they were taken out of the sequence. But suppose 1) that these references to those "inside the tent" and "outside the tent" meant the Jerusalem faction of the early Christian community versus the diaspora that included pagan participants; and 2) that the sacrifice in the sanctuary also referred to the cultural Greco-Roman custom of holding a feast, a banquet, or an animal

139

sacrifice in order to restore right relationships among gods, patrons, and clients.

The Roman sacrifice was the public ritual that preceded a private banquet or feast. The animal would be slaughtered by the priest, and its blood poured onto the altar of whatever god was being honored. Then the meat would be given to the one who paid for the sacrifice, and would be eaten by the clients invited to the feast. Crossan says, "Public sacrifices did not so much distinguish between immortal gods and mortal humans as announce and reinforce the hierarchy from the gods down along a scale of human participants and spectators . . . strengthening the bonds of loyalty among the many little pyramids built atop each other and made up of layers and layers of patrons and clients."[38]

The preacher uses a fascinating metaphor in verses 10-14. He reminds his listeners that the blood of animals sacrificed by the priests ("those who officiate in the tent," – or tabernacle) is poured on the altar as a sacrifice for sin, while the bodies of the animals sacrificed by the priests are burned outside the camp, not eaten, as in the Roman patronage system. Jesus was killed outside the camp, the preacher says, and his blood made the people holy. The preacher tells us to also go "outside the camp" and put ourselves in the same position Jesus put himself in. Namely, in opposition to Empire, in solidarity with those in prison, and even prepared to accept torture and death. We can do that because Jesus showed us how to do it.

Scholarship's best guess about what actually happened to Jesus is that he was probably crucified outside the city in a mass execution. Paul teaches that Jesus's death (his "blood") is the signal that the general resurrection of the martyrs has begun, and that the Kingdom of God is here now. All we have to do is choose to participate. This is way beyond forgiveness of petty sin. "Honoring marriage" and calling attention to your own humility are hardly radical acts.

The alternative readings for Proper 17 – i.e., the ones that do not support the thrust of the New Testament readings – are from Jeremiah and Psalm 81. These are perfect readings for

---

[38]Ibid., 298.

thundering about how the leaders of the people have abandoned their own history under the leadership of God. God rants: "Be appalled, O heavens, at this, be shocked, be utterly desolate . . . for my people have committed two evils: they have forsaken me, the fountain of living water, and dug out cisterns for themselves, cracked cisterns that can hold no water." Psalm 81 calls for the people to turn back: "O Israel, if you would only listen to me! . . . Open your mouth wide and I will fill it. But my people did not listen to my voice; . . . So I gave them over to their stubborn hearts, to follow their own counsels. . . . O . . . that Israel would walk in my ways! Then I would . . . feed you with the finest of the wheat, and with honey from the rock I would satisfy you."

Here is a call from God/dess to trust in the realm that sustains us, instead of selling out to the Empire, whose policies hold no water, and whose sacrifices do not restore right relationship (righteousness) with anything.

Proper 18
The Prisoner of Empire

Jeremiah 18:1-11; Psalm 139:1-6, 13-18;
Deuteronomy 30:15-20; Psalm 1; Philemon; Luke 14:25-33

What a hodge podge of readings this week. Something for everyone: The sin of idolatry seems to be the most prevalent (Deuteronomy, Jeremiah); then there is the nature of God as all-knowing, all-nurturing security (Psalm 139); Psalm 1 says there are two kinds of people in the world, and God makes the good prosper, and the wicked perish; and good ol' Luke reduces Jesus's radical cost of discipleship to prudent cost-benefit analysis for economic development, and advance planning for war in case negotiation fails.

Then there is the letter to Philemon, regarding his runaway slave Onesimus.[39] John Dominic Crossan analyzes this letter in *In Search of Paul*, pp. 107-110. Onesimus has appealed for intervention in his case to Paul, who is in a Roman prison, chained to a personal guard. Crossan imagines that the reason for Onesimus running away must not be too critical, or Onesimus would never have put his life and Paul's life in mortal danger by coming to him for help. There is no way to know exactly what the circumstances were. We do know that Paul is being very diplomatic toward Philemon, who is the host for the Christian community in Colossae. Onesimus appears briefly in Colossians 4:9, but we don't know whether Paul wrote to Philemon before or after that reference. Crossan says that what is crucial to Paul is that among Christians there is neither slave nor free. Paul works very hard to get Philemon to agree to set Onesimus free out of a sense of justice and right relationship among the members of the Christian community. As the notes point out in the NRSV, "The result is a masterpiece of church diplomacy."[40]

---

[39]Ibid., 107-110.

[40]National Council of Churches, *The Harper Collins Study Bible*, 2247.

Crossan poses the following: "[Paul's] implicit principle extends across all of Christianity . . . all Christians are equal with one another. . . . But, says our modern sensibility, that's only about Christians, not about pagans, not about the world at large, not about abstract and universal principles of freedom and democracy. . . . Paul says nothing about equal creation or inalienable rights, but imagine this conversation: Do you think, Paul, that all Christians should be equal? *Yes, of course.* Then do you think, Paul, that it is God's will for all people to be equal with one another? *Well, let me think about that one for a while, and in the meantime, you think about equality in Christ.*"[41]

So let's think about *equality in Christ.* Luke – and most of Western and church history – has missed the point. Jesus, and his interpreter Paul, are not talking about economics, whether in these readings or elsewhere. No way is the normalcy of civilization's pious reminder to "give up all you own" anywhere close to the radicality of Jesus's warning that to follow in his footsteps into the Kingdom of God means that you will become estranged from home, family, social support, and even be killed. Paul's life is already in jeopardy before Onesimus appears on the scene with his first century conundrum: How can he be an equal brother in Christ to Philemon and still be a slave? Paul has to tread carefully as he points out to Philemon that in order to be a part of the Kingdom of God as illustrated by the life of Jesus, he has to give up his lucrative ownership of another human being. Philemon has to be convinced that God's distributive justice-compassion requires him to act in opposition to the customs, if not the laws, of Rome.

If the Christ is a metaphor for a cosmic spirit of distributive justice-compassion, the Buddha nature, even the universe itself,[42] then Crossan's imagined conversation with Paul can have only one outcome: All people are equal. More, all of creation is equal in worthiness, demanding an equal chance at sustainable life. Respect for the natural world and the consequences of natural processes leads to a balance that can

---

[41]Crossan and Reed, *In Search of Paul*, 110.

[42]See Fox, *The Coming of the Cosmic Christ.*

143

only result in justice-compassion for all life forms. The cost of following Jesus's way in the service of that spirit may include ostracism and exile from family, tradition, community.

Here is where the rest of the readings comes into play – especially the warnings against idolatry. Idolatry is not only worshiping an image of god made of gold or silver or wood or stone. Idolatry means that material values have replaced spiritual values as the guiding force. Society has fallen out of the sustainable balance of the natural order. This problem is hardly new. Crossan calls it the "normalcy of civilization," which inevitably results in retributive imperial rule.

In Spotsylvania County, Virginia, yet another tragedy unfolded when a 16-year old boy murdered his sister, and left her two toddlers locked with the corpse for 24 hours inside what can only be called a hovel where they lived. The traumatized father mumbled something to the "live" interviewer about how the boy had been on depression medication. The distraught mother could only shriek that God had wanted someone dead that day, so he picked her daughter.

There is no excuse for a twenty-first century society that prides itself on justice and fairness, and claims it was founded on enlightenment, to allow people to become so enslaved in physical, material, spiritual ignorance. For people to be exiled to such ignorance is the result of the idolatry of a church and society that has sold out to Empire. Jeremiah goes on past the required reading (18:13-16): "Ask among the nations: Who has heard of the like of this? . . . My people have forgotten me . . . and have gone into bypaths, not the highway, making their land a horror."

God is inescapable, says Psalm 139. The poet speaks of God's knowledge as intimate and nurturing, beginning before birth. Deuteronomy 30:15-20 says that God sets before the people the ways of life and prosperity versus death and adversity. If the people obey God's commandments, they will prosper. If they turn to other gods, if they replace God's justice-compassion with their own selfishness, they will perish. In the potter's house that Jeremiah visits in the time of the exile to Babylon, the wheel spins and God shapes evil against those who refuse to turn back to God's ways. Jeremiah's point is a universal point that applies wherever God's people may be. For a society to insist it can prosper outside of God's justice-compassion is as futile as if the clay were to tell the potter it will keep its own shape.

Undoubtedly, the county authorities will try the boy as an adult for premeditated murder, and because Virginia is a death penalty state, he will pay. The defense will argue he was off his meds, and therefore not criminally responsible. So the argument will go, and we will likely not know the outcome until months later, when the local news affiliate follows up on the sensational murder and discovers that the required retribution has been accomplished.

So let's think again about *equality in Christ*. Where is the prisoner of the Empire to whom people enslaved by such profound systemic injustice can run to claim asylum?

Proper 19
Piety versus Covenant

Jeremiah 4:11-12, 22-28; Exodus 32:7-14; Psalm 14;
Psalm 51:1-10; 1 Timothy 1:12-17; Luke 15:1-10

Western Christian tradition claims that the New Testament is the actualization, or the culmination of the Old Testament: The new covenant with Jesus Christ replaces the old one of Moses. This would seem to be borne out by the readings, which juxtapose the prophets or the books of Moses with the letters of Paul to the newly established churches in the diaspora. But the letters to Timothy, which are recommended reading for the next seven weeks, and 2 Thessalonians and Colossians, which will finish out Year C, are all either definitely pseudo-Paul, or under enough suspicion by scholars that including them in that category is a reasonable position to take. Along with Luke – which is nearly all about justifying normal social behavior in the Roman world – these readings fall far short of any kind of actualization or fulfillment of the radicality of God's relationship with God's people, whether expressed through the story (Exodus, Deuteronomy), or the strenuous objections of the prophets to any acceptance of the laws, customs, gods, or morality of the surrounding or conquering civilizations.

In short, the remainder of Year C contrasts Covenant with the God of distributive justice, and the compliant piety of the comfortable citizens of the Empire.

The early Christian movement – especially Luke – was most interested in "repentance" and conversion. "Repentance" in this context might mean turning away from petty sin and giving alms to the poor, or doing good works, or acting fairly in business matters. However, "repentance" also can mean conversion from either traditional Judaism or paganism to the new Christian way. In the parables of the lost sheep and the lost coin, Luke is maintaining that no soul is insignificant; that God will not stop until the lost one – the pagan or the traditional Jew – is found. By the time Luke was writing his version of the story of Jesus, Greek concepts about the nature of the soul and the afterlife were very much in vogue among the shop keepers

146

and participants in the more economically secure strata of Mediterranean society. Jesus's original message – as interpreted by authentic Paul – of the immediacy of the Kingdom of God and the invitation to participate in that Kingdom here and now has already been forgotten.

Even though Jesus probably would have told a story in which a shepherd against all wisdom leaves ninety-nine sheep unprotected on a hillside while he goes in search of the one who is lost, the context of that story is impossible to know, and the meaning has been swallowed up in the piety of the early Christian movement. Jesus was interested in distributive justice and the kind of God that loves and seeks out those who are lost to unjust systems, not saving souls for some kind of afterlife. A more fitting Old Testament reading to accompany Luke's point might be Genesis 18:16-33, where Abraham negotiates the salvation of the city of Sodom for the sake of ten righteous (just) men. But that's not what the order of readings suggests. The Old Testament readings have nothing in common with the story in Luke, nor with 1 Timothy.

In the reading from 1 Timothy, the writer (not Paul) is confirming Luke's favorite theme of repentance and conversion. "I received mercy because I had acted ignorantly in unbelief. . . . Christ Jesus came into the world to save sinners . . . [and] for that very reason I received mercy so that . . . Jesus Christ might display the utmost patience, making me an example to those who would come to believe in him for eternal life." Jesus is the shepherd who saves the one who repents.

Psalm 51 is a prayer for cleansing and pardon, so Psalm 51, plus Luke, plus First Timothy are the readings most pertinent to the survival of the early Christian community, caught up in the Roman social system described by John Dominic Crossan as "piety, war, victory, peace." In order for Empire to achieve peace, the people must conform to official piety, they must support wars that conquer new territories, so that military victory can then bring peace (Pax Romana) to the known world. First century piety was defined by family values, the economic system of patronage, and public religion, which deified Caesar. So long as the Christians concentrated on ministry to the poor and the condition of the afterlife of the soul, the Empire couldn't care less about the teachings of Jesus. So long as the Jewish/Christian God was one of many lesser gods in the Roman pantheon, the God-Emperor Caesar would ignore it. Luke's Jesus is not going to overthrow the Roman social order.

But what about those "alternative" readings from Jeremiah and Exodus? The creators of the RCL allow for the minister or priest or spiritual leader to choose which of the readings is most pertinent to the community. For those who subscribe to the traditional teachings of the Western church, Jeremiah, the Psalms, and the story of the golden calf from Exodus are all cautionary readings about the jealousy of the Hebrew God, who will destroy all those who do not believe in him. Under that interpretation, the loving, forgiving, saving God (Christ) of the New Testament clearly actualizes the tribal, unforgiving war god of the Old Testament. Or, if the spiritual leader of the traditional faith community is concerned with "sin" – in the form of "idolatry" such as gambling, pornography, or materialism; or the decline of "family values" – in the form of same-sex marriage, abortion, or birth control, then Jeremiah's condemnation is right-on: "They are skilled in doing evil, but do not know how to do good," and his warning: "For thus says the Lord: The whole land shall be a desolation; . . . for I have spoken, I have purposed; I have not relented nor will I turn back."

The cherry-picking of Jeremiah and Exodus misses the point. In these readings, God is angry that the people either have already or may soon choose to follow the ways of the other tribal gods that surround them. The problem is not that they are not gods. In premodern times, multiple gods were normal. The problem is that those other gods do not stand for distributive justice-compassion. True, the early Israelites' God brought justice-compassion to his own people, and destruction to outsiders. But justice is the operative word, and the people of Israel and Israel's God were delighted when their enemies realized that.

And so it is today. With any social "sin" that is held up for repentance by the preachers of the traditional Christian religion, the underlying condition is injustice. We in the twenty-first century (as in the first century) can choose Covenant with God's Kingdom of justice-compassion as illustrated in the words and deeds of Jesus, or compliance with the easy piety of Empire, which allows us to bash gays, oppress women, persecute immigrants, and launch "signature" drone strikes that target anyone who looks like the enemy.[43]

---

[43]See Klaidman, *Kill or Capture.*

Proper 20
The Joke's on Us: Piety versus Covenant 2

Jeremiah 8:18-9:1; Amos 8:4-7; Psalm 79:1-9; Psalm 113;
1 Timothy 2:1-7; Luke 16:1-13

For arcane reasons, probably long forgotten by the Elves who put together the modern RCL, the readings for this Proper 20 echo the agricultural wheel of the year in the Northern hemisphere. Late September brings Mabon – the fall equinox. It is a time of balance in the Earth's eco-system, as the sun appears to rise due east, and set due west. This is the time of the second harvest, which lasts until November 1. It is the time of reckoning, of tallying, of accounting, and of balance sheets.

The parable of the shrewd manager is baffling, and Luke apparently was the only one to record that bafflement, as he once again tries to interpret Jesus's outrageous joke in terms of conventional piety. The second meaning of "pious" in the American Edition of the *Oxford Dictionary,* is "hypocritically virtuous." How else to describe the attitude of Luke's "children of light" (the Christian community Luke was writing for), who take worse care of their own than do the "children of this world," who lie, cheat, and steal? Luke works hard at twisting the story around to some kind of "Kingdom of God" metaphor, but it sounds more like honor among thieves: "So if you couldn't be trusted with ill-gotten gain, who will trust you with real wealth?"[44]

The sanctimonius writer of the letter to Timothy is long lost to the ransom theory of the atonement. Jesus's story about the shrewd manager has nothing to do with ransom, nor with atonement. Suppose Jesus is not talking about the nature of the Kingdom of God, but is making fun of the patronage system that the Roman world participated in? The Jesus Seminar scholars end the actual words of Jesus with verse 8a. "The master praised the dishonest manager because he had acted shrewdly." Luke's tortured attempt at clarification follows, until

---

[44]Funk, Hoover, and the Jesus Seminar, *The Five Gospels*, 358.

verse 13, which the Seminar agreed Jesus may have said at some time, but was probably not originally attached to the story: "No servant can be a slave to two masters. . . ."

Let's lift verses 1-8a out and imagine the scene as Jesus and his followers and friends lounge around a fire on the beach, finishing off the last of the fish they poached from the lake. Maybe one of them just got sacked from his job as a steward for one of the land-owners, who then awarded his job to the nephew of a local Roman official in exchange for a contract on the soon-to-be harvested wheat crop. The cascade of contracts stemming from the wheat crop that the unfortunate steward had already arranged for are now all null and void. His family now has to rely solely on his wife's skill as a weaver to supply the means for food, clothing, and shelter, and the wool she was to have acquired was part of that whole fabric of deals. The steward is looking death in the face.

Jesus's joke points out the corruption and injustice in the whole system of patronage when the master – rather than prosecuting the manager for fraud – rewards him: A first century version of the twenty-first century Enron scandal, which left hundreds of employees out of work, out of savings, and out of luck. The difference is, in the twenty-first century it's not a joke, it's a crime. Jesus would not have left our unfortunate wayfaring steward stuck in a painful irony. Perhaps he reminded him that God showers rain on the grass that is here today and tomorrow is tossed into the fire, or quoted Psalm 113: "Who is like the Lord our God . . . who . . . raises the poor from the dust, and lifts the needy from the ash heap?" After all, Jesus might have said, "You can't be enslaved to both God and a bank account."

Meanwhile, back in the Old Testament covenant with God's distributive justice, Jeremiah laments: "The harvest is past, the summer is ended, and we are not saved." The people continue to reject God's distributive justice and instead follow the gods of the exile. Jeremiah knows that even though the harvest was good, the people will be destroyed. They are too ready to trade justice for security, and false morality for personal gain. Amos confirms: "Hear this, you that trample on the needy, and bring to ruin the poor of the land, saying, 'when

151

will the new moon be over so that we may sell grain and the sabbath so that we may offer wheat for sale? . . we will . . . practice deceit with false balances, buying the poor for silver and the needy for a pair of sandals, and selling the sweepings of the wheat' . . . but the Lord will not forget any of their deeds."

Recently, lenders in the U.S. housing market played fast and loose with credit, luring the unwary and the marginally qualified with low "teaser" interest rates, then bundling these higher-risk loans into packages that were sold in the global financial market place. When the poorly-secured loans began to default, the effects were felt world-wide. We don't need an interventionist "god" to crook a finger and send the U.S. economy into pre-recession panic. When humans act unethically, the consequences are not always immediate, but they are certain.

The choice is ours: Empire, with its shallow piety, war, victory, and then an uneasy peace based on the capriciousness of the whole system; or participation in Covenant with the order of the universe, which for humanity, works in a context of nonviolence and distributive justice-compassion, leading to the kind of secure peace that is not dependent on economic or political conditions.

Proper 21
The Field at Anathoth:
Piety versus Covenant 3

1 Timothy 6:6-19; Luke 16:19-31; Amos 6:1a, 4-7; Psalm 146; Jeremiah 32:1-3a, 6-15; Psalm 91:1-6, 14-16

The readings from Timothy and Luke are so full of traditional piety that any meaning other than hypocritical virtuousness is difficult to discern. After condemning the rich, who fall away from the faith and get into trouble, the writer of the letter to Timothy backs off and advises that if you're already rich, then your task is to be "rich in good works" so that you can store up points for the future, when Jesus returns, and you can "take hold of the life that really is life."

In the first quarter of the fourteenth century, Meister Eckhart said in a sermon, "Behold how all those people are merchants who shun great sins and would like to be good and do good deeds in God's honor. . . . They do these things so that our Lord may give them something, or so that God may do something dear to them. All these people are merchants. This is more or less to be understood since they wish to give one thing in return for another. . . ."[45] Eckhart was preaching on the story in Matthew 21 about the time Jesus drove the money changers out of the temple. Eckhart is saying that the temple is the soul of a person. He says, "Who were the people, who were buying and selling in the temple, and who are they still? Now listen to me closely! I shall preach now without exception only about good people."

The "good people" he is preaching to are likely to be thinking in terms of tit for tat with God, perhaps on the order of what the writer of Timothy is suggesting. Somehow, some way, "God" rewards the good and punishes the bad in the next life. Luke's reversal of fortune story about the rich man and Lazarus is satisfying because Luke is very clear that the poor man goes directly to heaven, while the rich man gets the karma he earned

---

[45]Fox *Breakthrough* Sermon 32.

153

with his indifference to the plight of the poor. Such moralism might have made the story salvageable, but then Luke gets sidetracked into a diatribe against those who refuse to believe the story about Jesus's resurrection, which could easily turn into support for anti-Semitism. This is the easy piety of Empire, not the distributive justice-compassion of Covenant

The Elves manage to put Amos into the same context – which is outrageous. Amos is probably the most militant of all the prophets. ("Let justice roll down like the waters, and righteousness like an ever-flowing stream!") Yet they contrive to have Amos support the merchant's convention: "Alas for those who lie on beds of ivory . . and eat lambs from the flock . . . who sing idle songs . . . who drink wine from bowls, and anoint themselves with the finest oils, but are not grieved over the ruin of Joseph! Therefore they shall now be the first to go into exile."

The normalcy of twenty-first century civilization – world-wide – is that same merchant mentality that Meister Eckhart preached about in the fourteenth century, but with a particularly postmodern twist. Justice-compassion is bad for business and a detriment to political power. The only way to get any respect is to make money. "Working" means making money, not fulfilling vocation or actualizing art or natural talent. One would think that the work that should be most valuable to society would be child care and health care (that's *care*, not *insurance*). Instead, the most money is made by commercial corporations, male sports stars, and the military-industrial complex, which includes Big Oil, conventional energy, and all the businesses that support them. To make matters worse, taxes – which should go to assure social well-being – are levied most heavily on those most vulnerable: the working poor, small business, and the middle class; and they are used to support the Empire model of piety, war, victory.

Contrary to Luke and the writer of 1 Timothy, Jesus was teaching about this life, and participating in God's Kingdom here and now (Covenant). The trick is to discover trust in that Covenant regardless of the circumstances. As a demonstration of his trust in the covenant with God, the prophet Jeremiah buys a field at Anathoth on the eve of the Babylonian conquest, when

154

the people of Israel are facing certain exile and slavery. This is a defiant – even a subversive – act in the face of Empire. He honors the Mosaic law spelled out in Leviticus 25:25-28, that allows – perhaps obliges – a family member to "redeem" land that is in danger of being lost to debt. With the Babylonians at the gates of Jerusalem, Jeremiah agrees to buy the field. It is an act of trust that the people will return by the Jubilee Year, fifty years after the sale is arranged, and the land will then be restored to them.

What is the field at Anathoth today?

What is the postmodern radical act of trust in Covenant with the rhythm of the universe? Leviticus 25 also speaks of the Sabbatical Year. Every seven years, there is to be complete rest for the land. How ironic that in the twenty-first century, Israeli farmers scramble to hire non-Jewish Palestinians to work their land during the Sabbath years – of which 2007 was one. Leviticus 25:6 does allow that the people "may eat what the land yields during its sabbath," but that is not meant to be a loophole for the merchant mentality to wriggle through. Here is plenty of opportunity for a radical return to Covenant.

And what of Christians, who believe that the Christ is the New Covenant? What is our field of Anathoth? Perhaps this: as individuals, to deliberately abandon self-interest as Jesus did; to extend distributive justice-compassion, not pay-back, in every situation. Collectively, to establish nonviolent solutions to the trouble spots exacerbated by the theology of Empire by replacing military might with medical personnel, teachers, food suppliers, and experts in sustainable living. Under such a Covenant, "You will not fear the terror of the night, or the arrow that flies by day, or the pestilence that stalks in the darkness, or the destruction that wastes at noonday. . . ."

Proper 22
Here We Go Round the Mulberry Tree

Luke 17:5-10; 2 Timothy 1:1-14; Lamentations 1:1-6;
Lamentations 3:19-26; Habakkuk 1:1-4, 2:1-4; Psalm 37:1-9;
Psalm 137

If you subscribe to the dogma that the Old Testament is fulfilled in the New, then the selection of readings for this Sunday might make some collective sense. Jeremiah and the writer of Lamentations were chronicling the disastrous Babylonian conquest of 586 B.C.E., when the people were forced into exile. The Lamentations passages are used in Jewish liturgy to commemorate the destruction of the Temple by the Roman emperor Titus in 70 C.E. In the Christian liturgical tradition, portions of Lamentations are read during Holy Week. Both interpretations have to do with a spiritual world that is transformed into an alien place overnight. In the Christian year, we are in the season that leads up to Advent, so it is appropriate to begin to look at exile and the promise of deliverance. The hymn, *O Come, O Come Immanuel and Ransom Captive Israel* is a favorite in Protestant churches for the Sundays in Advent, with its imagery of exile, and deliverance promised by the Messiah to come. Luke's reminder about the power of even the least amount of faith in Jesus, and his continuing theme of service to others keeps believers on track up to the end of the liturgical year; and of course, the writer of the second letter to Timothy urges continued courage in the struggle to spread the gospel of the Christ.

However, for twenty-first century exiles from traditional Christianity, the Elves have truly outdone themselves with non sequiturs for Proper 22. Luke's "faith" on the level of a mustard seed that would uproot the mulberry tree and plant it in the ocean is a lame substitute for the much more powerful proverb that faith will move the mountain into the sea. (Mark 11:23). As noted in *The Five Gospels:* "People in the ancient world thought the sky was held up by mountains that serve as pillars at the edge of the world. It is possible that moving mountains originally referred to the ability to *change the contours of the*

156

world." (Emphasis mine.)

Perhaps Luke used a different illustration for the proverb because by 95 C.E., rich, educated, Roman collaborators such as the ones Luke was writing for would have known that the sky was not held up by mountains at the edges of the world. Perhaps they thought those ancestors who invented the metaphor believed it literally. The scene conjured in the mind's eye as the mulberry tree is hurled into the ocean probably produced a few laughs around the banquet room, as Luke's guests reclined at dinner, trading intellectual witticisms, discussing the latest philosophical fad, and witnessing to their pious desire to serve rather than to be served.

One may be reminded of a certain twenty-first century world leader who found it amusing that nine million American children have no health insurance. "They have access to the best health care in the world," he said, with his crooked, ironic grin. "They can go to the emergency room!" Shades of Marie Antoinette, who said – in total ignorance of the circumstances of the poor – "Well, if they have no bread, let them eat cake!"

The New Roman Empire – Pax Americana – is brought to you by mercenaries such as Blackwater, founded by Erik Prince, a former Navy Seal and major contributor to the Republican Party, who enjoys "close ties" to Christian evangelical groups, and is a graduate of a Christian evangelical university. In his opening statement to the House Committee on Oversight and Government Reform, October 2, 2007, Mr. Prince praised the dedication of his employees, who put themselves in harm's way to protect America and America's people. His carefully nuanced, lawyer-vetted statement contrasted with a hearing held in February, when the wives of four Blackwater contractors who in 2004 were ambushed, murdered, and their bodies burned and hung from a bridge in Fallujah, Iraq, presented appalling testimony about the inner workings of this organization that only wants to serve the cause of freedom:

> In the case of Blackwater, the people making critical decisions are those in corporate America, whose focus is often on cutting costs and making a profit. . . . Blackwater gets paid for the number

157

of warm bodies it can put on the ground in certain locations throughout the world. If some are killed, it replaces them at a moment's notice. What Blackwater fails to realize is that the commodity it trades in is human life.[46]

Mr. Prince and the economic, social, and political systems that support Blackwater and other outsourced military proxies have sold out to the theology of Empire: piety, war, victory, peace. It is a false theology on several levels, but perhaps the most egregious in the web of lies is that piety, war, victory leads only to more piety, war, victory, and never peace. Participants in the theology of Empire include all branches of the U.S. Government: Executive, Legislative, Judicial; as well as the media; religious organizations; corporations; and individual citizens worldwide, who cannot, will not, dare not, and do not pay attention. These supporters and collaborators of Empire are the slaves in Luke's pious example, concentrating on the etiquette of seating and service, dinner and entertainment, instead of the radical abandonment of self-interest taught by Jesus. Luke is right. Such "faith" is truly the size of a mustard seed, and the joke is it doesn't come close to throwing the mulberry tree into the ocean, let alone changing the contours of this world.

When an interventionist God resides in the Temple and not as the spirit of covenant with justice-compassion in the heart, the result is alienation, powerlessness, and a shallow "belief" in impossibility. To paraphrase the desolation of true exile in Psalm 137, let us lean our guitars against the wall, and throw ourselves down on the banks of the Potomac River at the Watergate ampitheater across from the Pentagon, and weep. How can we possibly preach the Lord's distributive justice-compassion in a land where proxy wars are fought off-budget by "Christian" soldiers like Erik Prince? Prophets – such as Habakkuk and the writer of the Lamentations of Jeremiah, and Jeremiah himself – not only believed, they *knew* that God would act in real time to return the people to their land, and restore God's justice-compassion: "Do not fret because of the

---

[46]House of Representatives Hearing on February 7, 2007.

wicked: . . . Commit your way to the Lord; trust in him, and he will act. He will make your vindication shine like the light, and the justice of your cause like the noonday." Psalm 37:1-9.

Even in the midst of his unspeakable grief over the loss of Jerusalem, the writer of Lamentations trusts that God will make things right in the end. Remember that Jeremiah redeemed the field at Anathoth, and agreed to hold it until the proper owners returned. There is hope: "The steadfast love of the Lord never ceases . . . the Lord is good to those who wait for him, to the soul that seeks him. It is good that one should wait quietly for the salvation of the Lord." Lamentations 3:19-26.

That level of trust is an order of magnitude greater than Luke's "bibbety bobbety boo" that works whether you believe it or not. The kind of faith Jesus actually taught is trust in the power of choosing to participate in God's Kingdom of distributive justice-compassion, which changes the very contours of the world – or, in twenty-first century language, shifts the paradigm. The paradigm shift Jesus spoke of most often is the radical abandonment of self-interest individually, collectively, socially, politically, globally.

"Covenant" does not mean passive waiting for Godot. "Covenant" means active partnership in the ongoing work of distributive justice-compassion. "Covenant" means a never-ending reclaiming of spirit from the ease of complicity with the powers that seem to be. The writer of 2 Timothy, believe it or not, holds a clue in the cherry-picked verses for this Sunday: "[F]or God did not give us a spirit of cowardice, but rather a spirit of power and of love . . ." (2 Tim. 1:7). "How Long . . . shall I cry to you 'Violence!' and you will not save?" the prophet complains – and God answers: "Write the vision; make it plain on tablets so that a runner may read it. For there is still a vision for the appointed time . . . ." Habakkuk 2:2-3.

Proper 23
Exile from Covenant

Luke 17:11-19; 2 Kings 5:1-3, 7-15c; Jeremiah 29:1, 4-7;
Psalm 66:1-12; Psalm 111; 2 Timothy 2:8-15

The reading from 2 Timothy would seem to be the "optional" reading for this Sunday: "The saying is sure: If we have died with [Christ] we will also live with him; if we endure, we will also reign with him; if we deny him *he will also deny us*; if we are faithless, he remains faithful – for he cannot deny himself. . . . Do your best to present yourself to God as one approved by him . . . rightly explaining the word of truth" (emphasis mine). This is irredeemable gobbledegook. The Christ preached by the real Apostle Paul was an instrument of inclusive grace, not exclusive condemnation. The theology of Empire demands pious belief, and that's what we get from this writer. If the Apostle Paul's name had not been attached to it, perhaps it would not be part of the canon.

The scriptures to focus on this week are 2 Kings, Jeremiah, and good old Luke.

According to the scholars who put together *The Five Gospels*, the stories about Jesus curing lepers in both Mark and Luke are not based on any experience of Jesus's actual life or sayings. The story in Mark (1:40-45) illustrates Mark's fascination with the secret messiah, who continually denies who he is, and even gets angry at people who recognize him – such as the leper who ignores his request and tells everyone, so that Jesus is forced to focus his ministry in the countryside. Luke tops Mark's healing of one leper with the healing of ten – which would seem to bury Mark's concern with secrecy. Then Luke really pours on the piety. Not only is the foreigner the one who shows gratitude and praises God's power, but the foreigner is a Samaritan – a hated alien – who *believes* the Jesus story, in contrast to the ungrateful cynics in Jerusalem. Luke's point – and the point of the repeated reading from Proper 9 (2 Kings 5:1-3, 7-15c) – is trust in the healing power of God/Christ. In both stories, it is the foreigner who acts on faith.

Jeremiah's letter to the exiles in Babylon dashes any hopes for the early return predicted by false prophets. Instead of accepting the imperial god of their captors, the exiles must learn that they are still bound to the covenant with their own god, who will act with justice-compassion.

There are two sides to the coin labeled "foreigner." One is the captive, who is forcibly removed from the homeland. The other is the conqueror, who invades. One is the stranger in a strange land, struggling to come to terms with spiritual, political, economic exile. The other is the host – willing or unwilling – of the immigrant or exile who has arrived.

Much of our Planet today is living in exile, either physical or spiritual, and in many cases both. The Planet is changing, ecologically, and economically. There is increasingly no escape from the alienation of climate transformation, food shortages, water contamination, pandemic disease, and violence. Resentment, fear, anger, and retribution are on the rise worldwide. So we turn to strong-armed power in military juntas, dictatorships, ideologies, mistrust of the unfamiliar, blame, and terror – all the false prophets raised up in Babylon, who distract us and seduce us into the theology of Empire. When we succumb to that seduction, we force Covenant, nonviolence, and justice-compassion – God – into exile. The God of distributive justice-compassion has been driven out almost everywhere, along with exiles from Christian and other faiths who are unwilling to comply with piety, war, and victory in order to grab an illusive peace.

The profound truth in the story in 2 Kings and confirmed by Luke is that the hated alien is the one who trusts in Covenant, nonviolent justice-compassion, and peace with the exiled God. What we don't read in Proper 23 – just as we did not read it for Proper 9 – is the betrayal of that trust on the part of Elisha's servant Gehazi (2 Kings 5:19b-27). When Elisha declines to accept the gentile Naaman's gifts in exchange for his miraculous healing, Gehazi is scandalized. "As the Lord lives, I will run after him and get something out of him," he says. When he catches up with Naaman, he makes up a story about unexpected company that needs silver and clothing. Naaman not only complies with Elisha's supposed request, he doubles the amount asked for. Shades of Jesus's recommendation found in Matthew 5:40-41 that if the Roman occupier demands your shirt, give him your cloak, or if he demands you carry his bags one mile, go for two. The outsider Naaman is generous to a fault. The insider Gehazi is corrupted and therefore cursed by Elisha with the very same leprosy Naaman was cured of.

An "exile" is someone who has been forced to unwillingly leave home and country. Some would not consider political or economic immigrants, whether legal or illegal, as "exiles," arguing that leaving because of adverse government policies or for a desire to improve economic status do not fit the description. Paul Keim, in an essay on Living by the Word in *The Christian Century* (September 18, 2007) asks, "And what of those of us whose home is the immigrants' foreign land? How might this metaphor reshape the moral imagination of us "captors" who offer (or benefit from) labor without dignity and opportunity without hope?"

More and more local and county governments in the United States are seriously considering denying public services such as education and health care to those who are thought to be "illegal" aliens because they are considered to be panhandlers and parasites, who take unfair advantage of opportunity while giving nothing in return – "nothing" meaning the supposed non-payment of local and national taxes. "Aliens," the argument continues, illegal or legal, require their home language to be used by government and commercial services. This causes prices to rise for everything, as bi-lingual and cross-cultural teachers, receptionists, doctors, secretaries, and government and public service employees are increasingly necessary.

Article 25 of the Universal Declaration of Human Rights says that "Everyone has the right to a standard of living adequate for the health and well-being of himself and of his family, including food, clothing, housing and medical care and necessary social services, and the right to security in the event of unemployment, sickness, disability, widowhood, old age or other lack of livelihood in circumstances beyond his control." Article 26 says that "Everyone has the right to education. Education shall be free, at least in the elementary and fundamental stages. Elementary education shall be compulsory." The United States was instrumental in the formation of the language of the Declaration, which was adopted by the UN in 1948. But then the imperial legalistic hair-splitting began. Because it is a "Declaration," the U.S. Congress decided it did not need to act to ratify it. Once the Declaration was signed by the member states, individual treaties were developed that addressed specific articles in the declaration – such as the death penalty, child welfare, and torture, among others. Needless to say, the United States has not ratified any of the individual treaties that sprang from the original Declaration.

Jeremiah's letter from Jerusalem to the exiles in Babylon is clear that the alien in the alien land must settle in. Jeremiah advises them to "Build houses and live in them; plant gardens and eat what they produce. Take wives and have sons and daughters; take wives for your sons, and give your daughters in marriage, that they may bear sons and daughters; multiply there, and do not decrease. But seek the welfare of the city where I have sent you into exile, and pray to the Lord on its behalf, for in its welfare you will find your welfare." Eventually, as Jeremiah promises with his redemption of the field at Anathoth, the people will be allowed to return. But some will die in exile; some will choose to remain even when given the chance to return, because they have taken their God – their commitment to covenant – with them.

God is not "out there," or "back there," but is found in living the Covenant – trust in the Covenant, stepping out in the determination to act in radical denial of self-interest. Only then can the alien be accepted as one with us. Only then can we return from exile with our God.

Proper 24
Paradox and Participation

Jeremiah 31:27-34; Psalm 121; Genesis 32:22-31;
2 Timothy 3:14-4:5; Psalm 119:97-104; Luke 18:1-8

The remainder of Year C contrasts Covenant with the God of distributive justice, and the compliant piety of the comfortable citizens of the Empire. In the readings for Proper 24, Luke's angry Jesus berates the community that doubts whether God will deliver justice comparable to the Empire, where judgment is awarded to the one who is most politically persistent, and the writer of the second letter to Timothy is blind to the hypocrisy of dogmatic piety. Jesus's bitter joke is totally misconstrued by Luke. Rather than being an illustration of faith (belief) in God's answer to prayer – as Luke forces the parable to be – Jesus is saying that the Roman judges are so corrupt, they reward judgment to those who scream the loudest, and who threaten their reputations the most. If Jesus were to tell the joke today, it might be about the U.S. criminal "justice" system, which treats racist taunting by white children as "pranks," barely deserving a reprimand, but tries as adults for attempted murder the outraged black children who retaliate.

The commentary from *The Five Gospels* says, "[The corrupt Judge] decides in [the widow's] favor to be rid of her. He wants to avoid being harassed, perhaps to avoid having his honor or reputation beaten black-and-blue (such is the implication of the Greek term used here) by her continual coming to demand vindication." It is not the nature of the "Kingdom of God" that our wishes will eventually be granted if we persist in our petitions. That is the expectation of the citizens of Empire, which demands loyalty and piety, not integrity, and retribution, not distributive justice.

If there was a real Timothy who accompanied the real Paul on a couple of his trips around the Mediterranean, he must have been tempted to kill the messenger who delivered those two letters – the first century equivalent of twenty-first century email spam. Just because they have Paul's name attached, and just because there are a couple of paragraphs that might actually make sense in terms of following the Christian Way, is no reason to accept them as any kind of guide for Jesus's radical abandonment of self-interest. "For the time is coming when people will not put up with sound doctrine, but having itching ears, they will accumulate for themselves teachers to suit their own desires, and will turn away from listening to the truth and wander away to myths. As for you, always be sober, endure suffering, do the work of an evangelist, carry out your ministry fully" (2 Tim. 4:3-5.) This is fertile fodder for fundamentalist fantasy, which results in martyrdom and religious wars. "Sound doctrine" has meant belief in a premodern myth of a dying-rising god, suspension of disbelief in a literal, personal, interventionist God, and a literal reading of the Bible that ignores postmodern cosmology and the struggle for relationship with the divine that goes back to Jacob.

The Genesis story is set up to be the prequel to the admonition to "endure suffering, do the work of an evangelist, carry out your ministry fully," just like Jacob, who ends up with a dislocated hip in his fight with God. The classic 1947 re-write of the Bible for children by Jesse Lyman Hurlbut tells the story this way:

> And while Jacob was alone, he felt that a man had taken hold of him, and Jacob wrestled with this strange man all the night. And *the man was an angel from God.* They wrestled so hard, that *Jacob's thigh was strained in the struggle. . . .* Then the angel said: "Your name shall no more be called Jacob, but Israel, that is 'He who wrestles with God.' For you have wrestled with God and have *won the victory.*" And the angel blessed him there. And the sun rose as the angel left him; and Jacob gave a name to that place. He called it Peniel, or Penuel, words which in the language that Jacob spoke mean *"The Face of God."* "For," said Jacob, "I have met God face to face." And after this *Jacob was lame, for in the wrestle he had strained his thigh.* (Emphasis mine.)

The story is watered down, not only by Hurlbut for

children, but for anyone who does not take seriously the Old Testament stories, which are foundational myths about the history of the Hebrew people and their relationship with their God. In the usual interpretation, the man who wrestles with Jacob is not God, but an angel from God; Jacob has won the victory and becomes (in the King James Version) a "prince" of his people, just as Jesus won the victory and became the Christ; Jacob sees God face-to-face, but Hurlbut leaves out the fact that having done so, he escapes with only a dislocated hip instead of losing his life.

The Jeremiah reading also seems to predestine the reading from 2 Timothy, if we accept the convention of prophecy and confirmation or actualization from the Old Testament to the New: "The days are surely coming, says the Lord, when I will sow the house of Israel and the house of Judah with the seed of humans and the seed of animals. And just as I have watched over them to pluck up and break down, to overthrow, destroy, and bring evil, so I will watch over them to build and to plant, says the Lord." Jeremiah 31:27-28. The section cherry-picked from Psalm 119 is further accompaniment to the pious posturing offered by the writer of 2 Timothy, who is blinded by dogma, and is unable to see the paradox, or hold the contradiction that is necessary for distributive justice-compassion (the "Kingdom" or realm of God) to hold sway. "Covenant" for that writer is a one-sided demand from God to humanity, somehow alchemically reconciled through the blood of the Christ.

But Jeremiah is actually reminding the people in exile that there is a time for every purpose: a time to plant, etc., and God will keep God's part of the bargain by providing protection and care. All the people need to do is live in justice-compassion, and trust the promise. See Psalm 121. Covenant for Jacob is the struggle for meaning in a relationship with "God." Not a corporeal god, but a paradox that includes strength and weakness, love and fear, good and evil, presence and absence. John Dominic Crossan proposes a *"kenotic* God, . . . a God whose gracious presence as free gift (Paul's *charis*) is the beating heart of the universe and does not need to threaten, to intervene, to punish, or to control. A God whose presence is justice and life, but whose absence is injustice and death."[47]

The ability to live centered in paradox is a sign of human spiritual and emotional maturity. The point is the struggle, not the intervention of supernatural power. The only way to engage the struggle and survive is to trust the process. Jacob encounters the human-divine paradox, and comes out of it surprised to be alive, wounded or diminished in physical power, yet whole. Covenant requires active participation in an ongoing mutual relationship with the God of Abraham, Isaac, Jacob, and – yes – Jesus. When Jesus speaks of the "Kingdom of God," he is talking about a realm – a paradigm – a parallel universe – where distributive justice-compassion rules. This "kingdom" is in direct opposition to the "empire" of Rome – and any other empire that comes down the pike of history, from the Babylonians to the British to the twenty-first century "pax Americana" promulgated by the policies foreign and domestic of U.S. presidents since (perhaps) Monroe.[48] The realm or "kingdom" Jesus was talking about is accessed by simply – and only – radically abandoning self-interest, and trusting the consequences of distributive justice-compassion.

---

[47]Crossan and Reed, *In Search of Paul*, 291.

[48]The fact that James Monroe declared the Western Hemisphere off-limits for European and/or British colonization may or may not have led to U.S. imperial hegemony; that is a point for political science debate, which is beyond the scope of this essay.

Proper 25
The Baby Went Out With the Bath
Protestant Reformation Sunday

Joel 2:23-32; Jeremiah 14:7-10, 19-22; Psalm 65;
Psalm 84:1-7; 2 Timothy 4:6-8, 16-18; Luke 18:9-14;
Sirach 35:12-17

The prophet Joel is the primary Old Testament reading of choice for Year C's Reformation Sunday, according to those pesky Elves. This book is nearly impossible to date – scholarly guesses range from 800 to 300 B.C.E. Joel (whoever he was) seems to be compiling an essay on the history of the Hebrew people and their relationship with God. ". . . [T]he invaders have come as punishment, . . . so Israel must repent by worship and fasting. The 'day of the Lord' predicted of old has come. . . . If the Israelites repent and return to the Lord, the army will leave and never again return. Their enemies will fall and their lands will be fertile forever." Perhaps these particular passages (2:28-32) were chosen because of their apocalyptic elements. For those who interpret the Old Testament as foreshadowing the New, and the New Testament as the actualization of the Old, these passages have traditionally been used to confirm judgment against all those who do not accept Jesus as Lord and Savior: "The sun shall be turned to darkness, and the moon to blood, before the great and terrible day of the Lord comes. Then everyone who calls on the name of the Lord shall be saved; for in Mount Zion and in Jerusalem there shall be those who escape, as the Lord has said, and among the survivors shall be those whom the Lord calls."

They also lend themselves to thundering against the corruption that led to the establishment of the Protestant Church in the West, and fall right into Luke's pious admonition: "Then for those who were confident of their own moral superiority and who held everyone else in contempt, [Jesus] had this parable. . . ." In the spirit of *midrash*, let's imagine Jesus – perhaps as the guest of Mary Magdalene's uncle – visiting the now nearly-derelict fishing village near the lighthouse tower on

Lake Galilee. Somehow, Mary's Uncle Mordecai of Magdala has managed to hold onto the better part of the relative wealth he enjoyed as a trader in fish before Herod Antipas built his rival Roman resort Tiberias, five miles away, and put the local fishing fleet out of business. Perhaps Uncle Mordecai has managed to become a successful supplier of the Romans' favorite fish sauce and caviar to the Herodian household without completely losing his integrity. Perhaps he is one of those who clandestinely supplies the Zealots and other members of the Jewish resistance with money and materiel.

With Jesus nearby, an opportunity arises for Mary to visit her family. A banquet is arranged, and Jesus is invited, along with as many of his rag-tag followers as can get away from their day jobs as fishing boat crews and managers of vineyards and olive orchards, owned by the collaborators with Rome. The feast has been consumed – with gratitude. The women have brought out the wine and the fruit, and before the conspirators get down to their real agenda, the jokes and the stories begin. After the wine jug has passed hand-to-hand among the recliners a couple of times, and the latest outrage perpetrated by the Romans has been discussed, Jesus says, "If you think the Romans are corrupt, listen to this: "Two men went up to the temple to pray. One was a Pharisee and the other a toll collector."

One of the women giggles: "Together?"

"Shhh!"

Jesus goes on: "The Pharisee stood up and prayed silently as follows: "I thank you, God, that I'm, not like everybody else – thieving, unjust, adulterous, and especially not like that toll collector over there."

"Right," somebody murmurs. "At least the Rabbis are on our side."

"'I fast twice a week,' the Pharisee says, 'I give tithes of everything that I acquire.'" But the toll collector stood off by himself and didn't even dare to look up to God. Instead he struck his chest in mourning and muttered, "'God have mercy on me, sinner that I am.'"

Jesus looks around at the quiet room. They know there is a punch line coming, but they can't imagine what it will be. The

Pharisee is living a righteous life, doing what he is supposed to do. The thieving, lying toll collector prevents us from landing our boats anywhere near the commercial piers at Tiberias unless we first consign three-quarters of the catch to him.

"Let me tell you," Jesus says, "The second man went back to his house acquitted, but the first one did not."

Acquitted?

The Five Gospels notes that in Luke's version of the story, the tax collector (not toll collector) is *justified* – a term used by the Apostle Paul in his arguments about how the death of Jesus has transformed humanity from subjection to the kind of retributive justice assured by the laws of empire to participation in the distributive justice-compassion of God's ongoing present-day kingdom. There was some argument among the scholars that perhaps the parable was not original with Jesus because the word "justified" is applied to individuals only after the early Christian movement was 50 years old. Luke probably had heard or read Paul's letters to the communities around the Mediterranean. In addition, Luke's interpretation frames the story in conventional piety: "For those who promote themselves will be demoted, but those who demote themselves will be promoted." When the word "acquitted" is used, as the Jesus Seminar scholars do, the story changes to a confounding illustration of distributive justice-compassion.

In the Kingdom or Realm of God, the self-righteous religious leader who tithes everything s/he acquires, cannot be acquitted of crimes against divinity. The toll collector, who is clearly complicit with the occupying forces, and participates in the ongoing corruption, is found not guilty. It's not about shameless self-promotion, as Luke dilutes the point. It's about realizing that I as the toll collector am caught in the web of unjust, imperial systems, and I cannot get out. The only salvation is the mercy – compassionate justice – grace – free gift – of God.

One of the reasons given for the sixteenth century Protestant Reformation of the Western Catholic Church is that the Church had become so corrupt that "sin" could be "forgiven" not through the "free gift" – *charis* – or "grace" of God as manifested by the death and resurrection of Jesus (the

170

"new covenant"), but through commercial deals in which gold or land or political influence (perhaps including arranged marriages and/or approved divorces) was the medium of exchange, and the more that was "donated" to the church, the greater the sin that could be ransomed. The normalcy of civilization had propelled the church – lock-step – into the Holy Roman Empire. The year was 1517.

If we look to our own century, what do we see in Luke's parable? I see a "Christian" church that cannot be acquitted of crimes against divinity; that supports violent solutions to problems; that insists upon its own self-interest first; that excludes, denigrates, and dehumanizes those who are of other religions, other races, other nationalities, other genders, who are poor, who are caught up in situations not of their own making; that seeks dominion over the earth itself, in flagrant misuse of humanity's unique position as the holder in the known universe of self-consciousness. I see a "Christian" church that has sold out to secular forces that seek domination and control through fear rather than a covenant partnership grounded in love.

Instead of drawing inspiration from the promise: "I will pour out my spirit on all flesh . . . your old men shall dream dreams, and your young men shall see visions," the Church claims the self-congratulatory bigotry found in the second letter to poor abused Timothy: "As for ME, I have kept the faith. . . . The Lord will rescue ME from every evil attack and save ME for the heavenly kingdom. To ME [oops, "him"] be the glory forever and ever amen."

But the Old Testament prophets Joel and Jeremiah are preaching "covenant" as a two-way street, a partnership between creator and created. Before the apocalyptic passage, Joel says, ""[B]e glad and rejoice in the Lord your God . . . for he has poured down for you abundant rain. . . . The threshing floors shall be full of grain, the vats shall overflow with wine and oil." God will keep God's part of the covenant: "I will repay you for the years that the swarming locust has eaten . . . [and for] my great army, which I sent against you." The signs for the coming day of the Lord – when God will keep his promise to pour out his spirit of distributive justice-compassion, are the "portents in the heavens and on the earth, blood and fire,

171

and columns of smoke." In the portions selected from Jeremiah, the people acknowledge that "our iniquities testify against us," but they then remind God that "you, O Lord, are in the midst of us, and we are called by your name," so you can't forsake us. "[R]emember and do not break your covenant with us." After all, "Can any idols of the nations bring rain? . . . We set our hope on you, for it is you who do all this."

In these postmodern times, when "God" is dead, and much of orthodox Christian belief is deemed irrelevant at best and destructive at worst, how can "covenant" be seriously discussed, let alone reclaimed as something to be returned to? Who is the party in the partnership that brings rain, and delivers us from the invading armies of locusts, whether in insect form or imperial uniform? An interventionist God is not an option. The covenant is with the *kenotic* (empty, no-thing) power whose presence is distributive justice-compassion and abundant life, and whose absence is injustice and death. The part of the bargain to be kept – as Jesus teaches in the parable of the Pharisee and the toll collector, and in all the other stories he told, as well as with his own death – is the radical denial of self-interest.

Five hundred years after Martin Luther, "Reformation" is not enough; "repentance" is not enough. It's time to haul the tub out back and dump the bath. The Baby hasn't been in it for some time.

Proper 26
Up a Tree Without a Sonic Screwdriver

Habakkuk 1:1-4; 2:1-4; Isaiah 1:10-18; Psalm 119:137-144;
Psalm 32:1-7; 2 Thessalonians 1:1-4, 11-12; Luke 19:1-10

The Year C denouement slogs on through Luke and
pseudo-Paul to the ultimate "Reign of Christ the King" coming
again on the last Sunday in November. The celebration of the
great Protestant Reformation and the Feast of All Saints began
the *parousia* of the Church Triumphant, before we start the
whole liturgical year over again, longing for deliverance from
sin, anticipating the birth of the One who will save us all at last.
It's a treadmill. Even the Elves have given up. Two of the
readings from the Old Testament Prophets for this week are
repeats: Habbakuk from just a month ago, and Isaiah from
Proper 14. Instead, let's substitute DVDs of the twenty-first
century version of the BBC 1970s cult hit series, *Dr. Who*. The
good Doctor has a boundless confidence in the ability of the
common, ordinary human to transform the world. Wherever the
TARDIS[49] takes him and his intrepid companion, the bad guys
who want to grab all the power and riches for themselves are
defeated, not by the Doctor, but by the insignificant, ordinary
person who sets things right – sometimes by sacrificing his or
her own life. The Doctor, armed only with a sonic screwdriver
(which reverses the polarity of neutron flow), sets up the
opportunity, but leaves to the individual the choice of whether
to take action. Much more riveting and illuminating than Luke's
tired pontificating about the toll collector Zacchaeus, who
promises to give away half his ill-gotten wealth to the poor, and
"If I have extorted anything from anyone I'll pay back four
times as much." Note it's only HALF his wealth. Note the IF.

Luke, writing 40 to 50 years after the death of Paul,
probably had no idea that nearly half of the letters to the
Christian communities around the Mediterranean Sea with the
apostle Paul's name attached to them were not written by Paul,

---

[49]TARDIS: a blue British phone box, disguising a Time
And Relative Distance In Space time travel machine.

and in fact contradict much of what the authentic Paul was suggesting about the meaning of the life and teachings of the historical Jesus. By the time Luke composed his pious tale about how Jesus saved the lost sinner Zacchaeus, the accommodation between the Christian Way and Rome's imperial theology (piety, war, victory, peace) was well advanced.

Crossan and Reed argue that the pseudo-Pauline letters are "an attempt to sanitize a social subversive, to domesticate a dissident apostle, and to make Christianity and Rome safe for one another."[50] From the point of view of Caesar there is no threat to the Empire if some fool toll collector wants to give half his wealth to the poor. Even better, if he makes his own restitution for extorting funds from local officials, he saves the expense of involving the imperial criminal justice system. It's a First-Century Faith-Based Initiative, designed to assure that the taxes paid by the citizens and the occupied territories go to support the Empire's program: "Romanization by urbanization for commercialization" (Crossan's words) in the first century Americanization (masquerading as Democratization) by militarization for economic exploitation in the twenty-first century.

Luke's "crowd,"criticizing Jesus for spending the day "with some sinner," is the establishment Luke was writing for: the educated spiritual leaders in Jerusalem, the middle- and upper-class citizenry who had successfully accommodated themselves to the Roman occupation. Zacchaeus plays to that crowd, and makes a public, political deal with Jesus to give up half his fortune and – in the true spirit of twenty-first century plausible deniability – he will *look into* whether he has extorted money. Incredibly, Jesus buys it, even though in an earlier story (Luke 18:18-25), when someone from the ruling class asked Luke's Jesus what he had to do to "inherit eternal life," Jesus told him to "sell everything you have and distribute the proceeds to the poor . . . and then come follow me." When the rich young ruler heard this, he was of course "very sad, for he was extremely rich." Luke's Jesus then says (and the historical

---

[50]Crossan and Reed, *In Search of Paul,* 106.

174

Jesus probably actually did say this at some point, although not in Luke's context): "It is easier for a camel to squeeze through a needle's eye than for a wealthy person to get into God's domain."

By making a deal with Zacchaeus, Luke's Jesus sells out his own ministry. He falls all over good ol' Zach. "Whatta Guy!" Jesus says. "This man is a real son of Abraham!" Zacchaeus reaches down from the tree and they high-five. "What did I tell you about myself?" Jesus brags. "The son of Adam came to seek out and to save what was lost!" and they set off for Zach's house.

Luke should have done a little cherry-picking from the prophet Habakkuk, who asks God: "Why do you make me see wrongdoing and look at trouble? Destruction and violence are before me; strife and contention arise, so the law becomes slack and justice never prevails. The wicked surround the righteous – therefore judgment comes forth perverted." The story about the short-statured, short-changing, cheating toll collector might have been very different. Luke's Jesus could have said, "You liar. No way I'm visiting your house. You're as bad as the money changers in the temple, who managed to transform a holy place into a safe haven for robbers." Ah, but then Luke would have written himself into a corner. Who are the robbers? Who are the robbed? Luke would have been waiting for the proverbial late-night knock on the door from the agents of the emperor.

That's the dilemma, of course. That's why Jesus's Way is so hard to actually follow. Taking care of the poor is the easy part – or maybe not, given the refusal of every level of government in the U.S. – from the officers running the neighborhood association through city, county, state, and national government in all branches – to redistribute wealth through fair taxes; assure health care (not commercial health insurance) for everyone; provide an education for all children that is free of political, social, religious ideology; and extend hospitality to the alien. The Elves may have gotten it right after all. Isaiah's indictment bears repeating:

"Hear the word of the Lord, you rulers of Sodom! Listen to the teachings of our God, you people of Gomorrah! What to me is the multitude of your sacrifices, says the Lord; . . . when you come to appear before me, who asked this from your hand? Trample my courts no more; bringing offerings is futile; incense is an abomination to me. New moon and sabbath and calling of convocation – I cannot endure solemn assemblies with iniquity. . . . When you stretch out your hands, I will hide my eyes from you; even though you make many prayers, I will not listen; your hands are full of blood. Wash yourselves; make yourselves clean; . . . cease to do evil, learn to do good; seek justice, rescue the oppressed, defend the orphan, plead for the widow. . . . If you are willing and obedient, you shall eat the good of the land; but if you refuse and rebel, you shall be devoured by the sword; for the mouth of the Lord has spoken."

Radical abandonment of self-interest sounds wonderful, romantic, revolutionary – until there is a real physical consequence to following through. Maybe that's why Jesus first asks if the leper desires healing before extending his power. Maybe the real cosmic joke that Dr. Who illustrates is that participation in the great work of nonviolent, distributive, justice-compassion is our choice. There is no intervening Savior/God, with or without a sonic screwdriver. There is only insignificant, ordinary humanity.

Proper 27
The Rush to Armageddon

Haggai 1:15b-2:9; Job 19:23-27a; Psalm 145:1-5, 17-21;
Psalm 98; Psalm 17:1-9; 2 Thessalonians 2:1-5, 13-17;
Luke 20:27-38

The readings for the last three "Propers" of Year C confirm the manifesto of the institutional Western Christian Church that Jesus's death and resurrection do NOT mean that the "day of the Lord" has arrived (2 Thessalonians 2:1-5). Only after Satan has been defeated in a great rebellion against God will Jesus return. Until that time, he has established the Church, which speaks for God in all matters. Anyone who preaches a different message is the "lawless one," who will be revealed as the anti-Christ – the last sign before the coming of the day of the Lord. The readings from the Old Testament are carefully selected to support this thesis. The stories from Luke are used to confirm both Jesus's miraculous, anointed conception, and the promise of ransom through Jesus's death for those who repent of their crimes: "today you will be with me in paradise." The epistles are all pseudo-Paul, and contradict authentic Paul's ecstatic and transformational insight that God's grace is free to all without caveat, and that God's great work of justice-compassion can hold sway if we only choose to accept the partnership offered and revealed by the life Jesus lived.

Covenant and distributive justice are trampled into the dust raised by the stampede into the Christmas shopping season. In the U.S., we'll stop for a moment to gorge on Thanksgiving turkey, then the doors at Walmart will open at 12:01 a.m. on Black Friday, and it's"Silent Night," and "Rudolph the Red-Nosed Reindeer," bringing lots of toys for good little girls and boys. But under the rush to Armageddon a faint protest may be heard. Please. Not so fast.

In this Sunday's readings, the question put to Luke's Jesus by the Sadducees (who did not believe in a resurrection) is the kind of typical, literal question trap, posed by pedantic debaters from time immemorial. Jesus takes the side of the Pharisees, who do believe in a resurrection, despite the fact that Luke's

Jesus rails against the Pharisees most of the time in Luke's stories. Of course, he had to agree with them in this instance, or risk denying the developing dogma of Luke's Christian community. Luke's Jesus seems to echo authentic Paul, who tells the church in Corinth that "it is better to marry than to be aflame with passion."[51] But Luke's Jesus is arguing that "those who are considered worthy of participating in the coming age . . . do not marry. They can no longer die, since they are [angels]. . . . So this is not the God of the dead, only of the living, since to him they are all alive." The idea that some are "considered worthy" implies that some are not, which flies in the face of Paul's opus magnus to the Romans, not to mention the first outraged, corrective, pastoral letter to the church in Corinth: "for as all die in Adam, so all will be made alive in Christ."

Paul was a mystic, not a literalist. Paul expected that God's realm of distributive justice-compassion would be established on earth within his lifetime, not at some future time. He also realized that the restoration of God's realm was an ongoing, present reality, caused by – made possible by – Jesus's death and resurrection. Luke and Luke's Jesus have already misunderstood Paul's extraordinary interpretation. For Luke, and increasingly, other influential voices in the first century Christian way, the Kingdom of God comes only after the defeat of evil. The stage is nearly set for violent apocalypticism.

The time has come in the liturgical year to revisit the questions that are the underlying watermark for these essays on the RCL: 1) What is the nature of God? Violent or nonviolent? 2) What is the nature of Jesus's message? Inclusive or exclusive? 3) What is faith? Literal belief, or trust in God's realm of distributive justice-compassion? 4) What is deliverance? Salvation from hell, or liberation from injustice?

The readings for Proper 27 (and for the remainder of Year C) seem to be shunting us into an imperial theology, whose foundation is to answer the four questions as violence, exclusiveness, literal belief (or suspension of disbelief), and salvation from hell. Like the orange barrels along the highway

---

[51] 1 Corinthians 7:9.

that guide us inexorably to a detour, these answers lead religion into piety, war, victory, and uneasy political peace. If we are not alert, we may lose our way, as the detour takes us farther and farther from our intended destination – especially at night, in the rain, in unfamiliar territory.

Discussion of the book of Job is a rich source for a Doctoral thesis. Classified as Wisdom Literature in Christian bibles, it explores the problem of evil and capricious injustice. But in the interest of verifying the apocalyptic dogma of the Western Christian church, the compilers of the RCL cherry-picked from Job the words used by G.F. Handel in his fabulous aria from his indescribable oratorio, *The Messiah,* "I Know that My Redeemer Liveth." It is a hymn to faith in the resurrected savior; it is in every soprano's repertoire for Easter and funeral services. So long as one takes the position that the New Testament is the actualization, the fruition, the ultimate evolutionary result of the Old, and does not ask questions about the context or the original intent, all is well.

But the "Redeemer" Job invokes in 19:25-27 may be a reference to the Canaanite god Baal, who dies and rises again with the agricultural seasons of the year. Perhaps he will intercede for Job with the High God who has abandoned him. The "Redeemer" is also the "avenger of blood," whose responsibility it is to pursue a killer and kill him in return (see Numbers 35.19), even if the death to be avenged was accidental (Deuteronomy 19.6). Job wants revenge. He has abandoned any notion of justice. Job is just like all of us, who stare real adversity in the face – war, famine, disease, death – and demand deliverance. Job has reverted to fundamentalism. He knows that the "Redeemer," the avenger of blood, will come after God himself.

Who will bring distributive justice to the world if God does not?

The prophet Haggai saw a great hope in the remnant of the Jewish people returning to Jerusalem from exile in Babylon in 539 B.C.E. They had begun rebuilding the temple, destroyed in 587 B.C.E., but the project had come to a halt. The prophet brought his oracle to the leadership, encouraging – exhorting – them to finish. "The latter splendor of this house shall be greater than the former, says the Lord of hosts; and in this place I will give prosperity." At the end of Haggai's collected oracles (not included in the readings), the prophet assures the community leaders that because the Temple has been restored, God will act to restore King David's messianic line, bringing God's justice-compassion and prosperity to the people and the land.

In orthodox theology, Job's "faith" in his "redeemer" and Haggai's prophecy find their fulfillment in the death and resurrection of the savior Christ Jesus, but only if the meaning of Job's frustrated cry for retribution is deliberately mis-read. Job's story might be reinterpreted as an allegory for Christian spiritual life if we include the end of Job's story (also – conveniently? – left out). After some time of false accusation by his friends, and ultimately blaming God for the evil that has befallen him, Job has an epiphany. He comes to an experience of God that is transforming: "I had heard of you by the hearing of the ear," Job says to God, "but now my eye sees you; therefore I despise myself, and repent in dust and ashes" (Job 42:5-6). Because of his transformation – his realization of a different experience of God that is outside the orthodox belief system and beyond the magical fundamentalism of his tribal faith – God tells Job that God will listen to Job's prayer on behalf of the friends who had so misunderstood the nature of God, and had therefore seriously misled Job.

Instead of interpreting these readings as a precursor of messianic salvation from Hell, culminating in the exclusive Body of Christ and the imperial violence of the Church Triumphant, perhaps the exiles from the traditional orthodoxy of the Christian church can use these metaphors to realize the radicality in Jesus's original message, and join the struggle to find the courage to live it out in covenant, nonviolence, justice-compassion, and the deep peace that passes all understanding.

Proper 28
Apocalypse Now?

Isaiah 65:17-25; Isaiah 12; Malachi 4:1-2a; Psalm 98;
2 Thessalonians 3:6-13; Luke 21:5-19

In an agricultural world, the season of early winter is one of uncertainty about the future, especially if the second harvest was not good, or if the rains are late or missing – as they have been in recent years. In 2007, the Governor of the State of Georgia arranged for "church and spiritual leaders" to gather in the State capitol building to pray for rain. Needless to say, this caught the attention of the separation of church and state watchdogs, and caused a collective eye-roll among those whose search for the meaning of "God" does not include the interventionist grandfather almighty. Nevertheless, it is fascinating how in a sophisticated, urbane, society that generally denies the existence of the natural world unless it is raining – and then complains – seasons of early Winter have brought drought, rampant staph infection among the general population, soaring oil prices, a collapsed housing market, a stock market in a permanent state of ricochet, an economy teetering on the brink of a long slide into recession, and prayer in the State house.

Apocalypse now?

The readings for Proper 28 are all about apocalyptic judgment, and retribution. The answers to the four questions that underlie this study – 1) What is the nature of God? Violent or nonviolent? 2) What is the nature of Jesus's message? Inclusive or exclusive? 3) What is faith? Literal belief, or trust in God's realm of distributive justice-compassion? 4) What is deliverance? Salvation from hell, or liberation from injustice? – are violence, exclusion, literal belief, and salvation from hell. These are the answers for full-scale, red alert, survival mode. These are always the answers when humans succumb to fear.

The reading from Luke is a portion of Luke's wholesale re-telling of Mark's "little apocalypse" in Mark 13. Biblical non-literalists know that Luke's gospel was written 20-30 years after Mark's gospel, and that Mark's gospel was written in the historical context of the destruction of Jerusalem by the Romans in 66-70 C.E. No way is any of this a memory of Jesus's words or actions. The retributive mood is nearly impossible to avoid. "Nation will rise up against nation and empire against empire," Luke's Jesus proclaims. "There will be major earthquakes and famines and plagues all over the place; there will be dreadful events and impressive portents from heaven"; not to mention persecutions, mass arrests, and betrayal by family and friends. But, Jesus promises, "Yet not a single hair on your head will be harmed. By your perseverance you will secure your lives."[52]

The cherry-picked prophet Malachi backs Jesus up: "The day is coming, burning like an oven, when all the arrogant and all evildoers will be stubble . . . but for you who revere my name, the sun of righteousness shall rise with healing in its wings. . . and you shall tread down the wicked . . . on the day when I act, says the Lord." The writer of 2 Thessalonians, following up from last week's diatribe about the "one destined for destruction," is very clear who the wicked are: "[K]eep away from believers who are living in idleness and not according to the tradition that they received from us . . . have nothing to do with them. . . ." The twentieth and twenty-first century hostile prejudice toward the poor finds its justification here: "Anyone unwilling to work should not eat . . . [they must] earn their own living." Perversely, in twenty-first century America, so-called "illegal immigrants," who are more than willing to work, are equally vilified. The still small voice of Isaiah's peaceable kingdom is drowned out in hysterical fear. Isaiah's – and Jesus's – astounding realm of distributive justice-compassion is nowhere to be found.

Malachi's coming messenger of justice – Elijah – has been conflated with John the Baptist and Jesus, according to Christian tradition, and the advent of the Christ is the first of the culminating events of history promised by the prophet. But Malachi is railing against corruption in the newly reconstructed temple in Jerusalem in the 6th century B.C.E. There are consequences for corruption, for abandoning the integrity and purity of the law. In Chapter 3:1-5, in words used by G.F.

---

[52]Funk, Hoover, and The Jesus Seminar, *The Five Gospels*, 382.

Handel in *Messiah*, Malachi says he is sending his messenger who will restore the covenant between God and the people. "But who can endure the day of his coming, and who can stand when he appears? For he is like a refiner's fire . . . and he will purify the descendants of Levi, and refine them . . . until they present offerings . . . in righteousness. . . . I will be swift to bear witness against . . . those who swear falsely, against those who oppress the hired workers in their wages, the widow and the orphan, against those who thrust aside the alien, and do not fear me, says the Lord of Hosts."

This is not revenge or retribution. The prophet is saying that the price to be paid for injustice is high. The revenge exacted for Al Qaeda's attack on New York City in 2001 has resulted in the death of hundreds of thousands of people who had nothing to do with the action on September 11, 2001, including U.S. armed forces personnel, victims of subway bombings in London and Madrid, and "2.5 percent of the population of Iraq. A matching percentage of the US population of 300 million would be 7.5 million—nearly the entire population of New York City."[53] Al Gore's "Inconvenient Truth" documents the consequences of ecological crimes against divinity such as the destruction of rainforests and the contamination of breeding grounds for birds, salmon, and shellfish, as well as the disappearance of diverse species of life.[54] "Species are currently going extinct at a faster rate than at any time in the past with the exception of cataclysmic encounters with extraterrestrial objects. A good proxy for the rate of extinction is the rate of growth in energy used by the human population. In other words, extinction rates are increasing in step with the product of population growth times the growth in affluence."[55]

Trust in the covenant means the conviction in the face of death itself that God's distributive justice-compassion will break through. Authentic Paul tells us it has broken through in the person of Jesus. But those who choose violence, exclusion,

---

[53]http://www.wsws.org/articles/2006/oct2006/iraq-o12.shtml.

[54]http://www.climatecrisis.net/.

[55]http://www.whole-systems.org/extinctions.html.

literal belief, and salvation from hell as the foundation myths for life look with glee to the coming apocalypse, and refuse to participate in actions to restore economic, social, racial, political, or environmental justice. The world is coming to an end, and the rapture is not far behind. Bomb Iran and bring it on. Who has time to care about "global warming"? Listen to the piety of 2 Thessalonians. Pay attention to the violent war prophesied (meaning "foretold") by Luke's Jesus. Wait for the coming victory, says cherry-picked Malachi, "the day that comes shall burn [the evildoers and] leave them neither root nor branch."

What fundamentalists of all varieties forget is that – as folk tales from all cultures tell us – there is always a way to change the prophecy, remove the curse, and avoid the apocalypse, whether the story is about a hero saving an enchanted maiden, or lifting a judgment against the land. In the postscript to Malachi, God says, "Lo, I will send you the prophet Elijah before the great and terrible day of the Lord comes. He will turn the hearts of children to their parents, so that I will not come and strike the land with a curse." There is always a choice to be made that will change the prophesied fate. Usually the choice involves giving up an idea about who the cursed one is by embracing the shadow – kissing the frog or marrying the hag – taking the perceived evil in, and incorporating and transforming it into wholeness.

Jesus's way of lifting the curse is to radically abandon self-interest, and to trust in the realm of distributive justice-compassion even though death is the result. That is the true meaning of the archetype of the Willing Sacrifice. When that choice is made, the blind see, the lame walk, the one who is lost is found, "the wolf and the lamb shall feed together, the lion shall eat straw like the ox, . . . they shall not hurt or destroy on all my holy mountain."

Proper 29
Speaking Truth to Power
(Reign of Christ/Christ the King)

Jeremiah 23:1-6; Psalm 46; Luke 1:68-79; Luke 23:33-43;
Colossians 1:11-20

We end the year with the prophecy that the reign of King David will be restored; with the birth of the messenger, John the Baptist; the forgiveness of sins for the penitent thief who is promised salvation from hell; and the declaration of the supremacy of Christ. Gerald Darring, the developer and webmaster of a Catholic website called *Theology Library*,[56] writes: "Christ the King rules from a throne made to execute criminals. His Kingdom is a place of death outside the city. His subjects are the poor and outcast, the rejected of this world. In this upside-down Kingdom, it is not the executor but the executed who will be with Christ in paradise." He then quotes the U.S. Catholic Bishops 1986 paper, *Economic Justice for All*: "What Jesus proclaims by word, he enacts in his ministry. . . . His mighty works symbolize that the reign of God is more powerful than evil, sickness, and the hardness of the human heart. He offers God's loving mercy to sinners, takes up the cause of those who suffered religious and social discrimination, and attacks the use of religion to avoid the demands of charity and justice."

As a friend once said, when the Catholics are good, they are very very good. They should be. In fact, there is no excuse for not nailing the truth about Jesus squarely, unequivocally, by abandoning the institutional self-interest of the Roman Catholic Church – and the same goes for the institutional self-interest of the Protestant denominations. The problem is the same one that all human institutions fall into, whether that institution is a neighborhood council, a religion, or a national governing system. That is, what John Dominic Crossan calls "the

---

[56]http://www.shc.edu/theolibrary/resources/about.htm.

normalcy of civilization," which leads inevitably to empire and empire's theology: piety, war, victory, peace.

Crossan is careful – in fact adamant – to say that this inevitable development is not because of human nature. Humans can choose whether to fall into empire or not. Humans can choose Covenant, nonviolence, justice-compassion, and peace instead. But it's easier to just go in the direction the horse is already going, and ride it into empire. It's far easier to let the jerk who's running the neighborhood association without consulting anyone or following the by-laws continue his or her self-serving course than to re-write the bylaws, then go door-to-door (in the face of unfriendly pit-bulls and the ubiquity of guns, legal or illegal), and convince seventy-five percent of the home-owners to agree, get involved, make the change, and throw the bum out. Expand that metaphor up through the levels of human social organizational complexity, and we have church and state hierarchies mired in corporate and individual sin with no hope of deliverance. Add fear to the mix and the likelihood increases by an order of magnitude that empire will be the result.

The greatest danger in celebrating a Sunday called "Christ the King" is the triumphalist, ego-bolstering, thrill of self-righteous conviction. Hymns for the Reign of Christ include: "*Jesus Shall Reign* (where'er the sun does its successive journeys run)"; "*Crown Him with Many Crowns* (the Lamb upon the throne)"; "*Rejoice the Lord is King*"; "*All Hail the Power of Jesus's Name*"; "*Ye Servants of God your Master Proclaim* (the name all victorious, of Jesus extol, his kingdom is glorious, he rules over all)." In the *United Methodist Hymnal* of 1989, the latest version available, the imperial theology of the church begins to bleed into the imperial theology of the state with the inclusion in the list of Julia Ward Howe's 1861 anthem, *The Battle Hymn of the Republic*.

All religious systems arise from a need to control behavior so that the family unit, the tribe, the city-state, the nation, can survive and thrive. The three major religions of the book – Judaism, Islam, and Christianity – have as their core the idea of creating a just and equitable society. The tension between the secular political needs of the state and the spiritual needs of individuals in their interactions with one another resulted in the U.S. in the principle – perhaps doctrine – of the separation of church and state, so that the state is enjoined from endorsing, supporting, or establishing any particular religion, and the church is enjoined from endorsing, supporting, or establishing any particular political agenda. The increasing involvement in secular political agendas of both the left and the right in U.S. Christianity has raised a debate about whether the separation of church and state ultimately means freedom OF religion, or freedom FROM religion. Certainly one's spiritual convictions inevitably inform one's secular, political actions. But when the self-interest of the secular State becomes indistinguishable from the self-interest of the Church, the result is crusades, pre-emptive wars, slavery, the oppression of women – all the appalling varieties of economic, social, political, and spiritual imperial injustice.

The purpose of the voyages of Christopher Columbus, seeking a political route to the economic riches of the Far East, became entwined with the belief of the Spanish Inquisition that in order for the world to be saved from sin, all people must accept Jesus Christ as their savior and lord. The result was the annihilation of entire indigenous cultures in North, Central, and South America. The prime contemporary example is the rise of Christian Zionism. "For Christian Zionists, the modern state of Israel is the fulfillment of God's covenant with Abraham and the center of [God's] action from now to the Second Coming of Christ and final battle of Armageddon, when the Antichrist will be defeated. But before this can occur, they say, biblical prophecy foretells the return of Jews from other countries; Israel's possession of all the land between the Euphrates and Nile rivers; and the rebuilding of the Jewish temple where a Muslim site, Dome of the Rock, now stands."[57]

This movement, aligned with the Christian Right, has influenced U.S. foreign policy, sometimes to the detriment of stated administration policy, which supports a Palestinian state. "[Some] observers say the Bush administration's tilt toward Israel in the Israeli-Palestinian dispute results from a coalition

---

[57]Lampman, "Mixing prophecy and politics."

of neoconservatives, the Jewish lobby AIPAC, and Christian Zionists – with the latter providing the grass-roots political punch as a prime Bush constituency."[58] The U.S. dependence on Middle Eastern oil and the state's desire to acquire that commodity for its own perceived political survival has become entangled with triumphalist religious literalism. The Middle East has been called a "powder keg" for many years. The convergence of church and state self-interests is a lighted fuse.

The readings for proper 29 are so closely aligned with traditional Christian dogma that it is nearly impossible to find any reference at all to covenant, nonviolence, justice-compassion, and peace. Jeremiah prophesies that because the leaders of the people have scattered them and failed to care for them [as happened when the Romans finally destroyed the Temple and the great diaspora began], God will raise up a king from the lineage of David. The "remnant" of the people [no longer a nation] will be returned to their homeland. This dovetails precisely with the Christian Zionist literalism that calls for all Jews to return to Israel; that set up the State of Israel in 1948; and that literally believes that Jesus will return as king, the Jews will convert to Christianity, and the New Jerusalem will be literally established, with the Temple literally rebuilt on the Temple Mount. Even Psalm 46, which is a hymn to trust in the strength of God to provide refuge, becomes an anthem to imperial power: "The Lord of hosts is with us; the God of Jacob is our refuge."

It is tempting to throw out the whole idea of "Christ the King Sunday" and use the Thanksgiving readings. [Deuteronomy 26:1-11; Psalm 100; Philippians 4:4-9; John 6:25-35] But no society on the Planet today can afford to ignore the literalists or the fundamentalists and hope they will just go away. Postmodern humanity is in the midst of a spiritual quest to re-imagine myth and metaphor based on a postmodern cosmology. Traditional, conservative, and orthodox believers, as well as secularists who insist that religion is irrelevant, are unable to participate in that quest because it calls into question the nature of God, the message of Jesus, the meaning of faith,

---

[58]Ibid.

and the possibility of deliverance from evil. Such a wholesale challenge to the meaning of life is insupportable except for the most courageous, or the ones with the most access to the leisure to pursue anything other than hand-to-mouth survival.

Even though most fundamentalists may be in the minority fringes of their respective religious traditions, many are in positions of political and religious power. Without an understanding of the belief systems to which they are anchored, and an informed and literate appreciation of scriptural tradition, speaking any kind of truth to that power is futile.

BIBLIOGRAPHY

BIBLIOGRAPHY

Angelou, Maya. *On the Pulse of Morning*. New York: Random House, 1993.

Armstrong, Karen. *The Battle for God: A History of Fundamentalism*. New York: Random House, 2000.

Barks, Coleman. *The Essential Rumi*. San Francisco: HarperSanFrancisco, 1995.

Bonhoeffer, Dietrich. *The Cost of Discipleship*. New York: MacMillan, 1976.

Borg, Marcus J. *Jesus: Uncovering the Life, Teachings, and Relevance of a Religious Revolutionary*. San Francisco: HarperOne, 2006.

Borg, Marcus J., and John Dominic Crossan. *The Last Week*. San Francisco: HarperSanFrancisco, 2006.

——. *The First Christmas: What the Gospels Really Teach About Jesus's Birth*. San Francisco: HarperOne, 2007.

Consultation on Common Texts. *Revised Common Lectionary*. Nashville: Abingdon Press, 1992.

Crossan, John Dominic. "First Light: Jesus and the Kingdom of God." *Living the Questions Participant Guide* (2009).

——. *God & Empire: Jesus Against Rome, Then and Now*. San Francisco: Harper Collins, 2007.

Crossan, John Dominic and Jonathan L. Reed. *In Search of Paul: How Jesus's Apostle Opposed Rome's Empire with God's Kingdom*. San Francisco: HarperSanFrancisco, 2004.

Dewey, Arthur J. *The Word in Time*. Berlin, WI: Liturgical Publications, Inc., 1990.

Dewey, Arthur J., Roy W. Hoover, Lane C. McGaughy, and Daryl D. Schmidt. *The Authentic Letters of Paul: A New Reading of Paul's Rhetoric and Meaning*. Salem, OR: Polebridge Press, 2010.

Eisenman, Robert. *James the Brother of Jesus*. New York: Penguin Books, 1997.

Ellis, E. Earle. "A Note on First Corinthians 10," Journal of Biblical Literature 76, no. 1 (March 1957): 53, http://www.jstor.org/stable/1364434

Fox, Matthew. *Original Blessing*. Santa Fe, NM: Bear & Company, 1983.

——. *The Coming of the Cosmic Christ*. San Francisco: HarperSanFrancisco, 1988.

——. *Breakthrough: Meister Eckhart's Creation Spirituality in New Translation*. New York: Doubleday, 1991.

——. *Sins of the Spirit, Blessings of the Flesh*. New York: Harmony Books, 1999.

Funk, Robert W., Roy W. Hoover, and The Jesus Seminar. *The Five Gospels*. San Francisco: HarperSanFrancisco, 1993.

House of Representatives Committee on Oversight and Government Reform: Hearing February 7, 2007 http://www.gpo.gov/fdsys/pkg/CHRG-110hhrg36546/pdf/CHRG-110hhrg36546.pdf

Hurlbut, Jesse L. *Hurlbut's Story of the Bible,* Original Edition. Chapel Hill: Yesterday's Classics, 2007.

Johnson Frykholm, Amy. "Reading the Rapture: Evangelical Worldviews and Left Behind," *The Fourth R* 20, no. 3 (May-June 2007), 3.

Kazantzakis, Nikos. *The Last Temptation of Christ*. New York: Simon and Shuster, 1960.

Klaidman, Daniel. *Kill or Capture: the War on Terror and the Soul of the Obama Presidency*. Boston: Houghton Mifflin Harcourt, 2012.

Lampman, Jane. "Mixing prophecy and politics." *The Christian Science Monitor*, July 7, 2004.

Levine, Amy-Jill. *The Misunderstood Jew: The Church and the Scandal of the Jewish Jesus*. San Francisco: HarperOne, 2006.

Loney, James. "118 Days: How I survived captivity in Iraq." *Sojourners Magazine* December 2006, 12.

National Council of Churches of Christ in the United States of America. *The Harper Collins Study Bible, New Revised Standard Version*. San Francisco: HarperCollins, 1989.

Priests for Equality. *The Inclusive Hebrew Scriptures, Vol. III: The Writings*. Lanham, MD: Altamira Press, 1999.

Sheehan, Thomas. "From Divinity to Infinity." In *The Once and Future Jesus,* by John Shelby Spong, Marcus Borg, Robert W. Funk, John Dominic Crossan, Karen King, Lloyd Geering, Gerd Luedemann, Thomas Sheehan, and Walter Wink. Santa Rosa, CA: Polebridge Press, 2000.

Spong, John Shelby. *Why Christianity Must Change or Die*. San Francisco: HarperCollins, 1998.
Starhawk. *The Earth Path*. San Francisco: HarperSanFrancisco 2004.
Swimme, Brian, and Thomas Berry. *The Universe Story*. San Francisco: HarperSanFrancisco, 1992.
Taylor, Jeremy. *The Living Labyrinth*. Mahwah, NJ: Paulist Press, 1998.

APPENDIX ONE

Eucharist

EUCHARIST

Matthew Fox's Creation Spirituality[59] calls us outside the orthodox theological boxes of fall-redemption and the ransom theory of the atonement. In a context of justice-compassion, a parent is nothing short of monstrous who would not only require that his or her own child be murdered so that others could be spared, but set the child up to that end. A god who governs creation like that can only invoke terror. Love is out of the question. Likewise, a remote god who intervenes based on someone's degree of righteousness is capricious at best. At the original end of the story of Job, having lost patience with his neighbors who try to convince him that he must have done something to deserve all the bad luck that has come his way, Job says, "If my land cries out against me, or its furrows weep together – if I ate its bounty without recompense, or gave its laborers reason to complain – let weeds flourish where once was wheat; let thistle take over the barley field!" Job 31:38-40.[60]

The Old Testament story of Abraham's near-sacrifice of his son Isaac is paired in the RCL with Romans 6. An angel speaks to Abraham as he is about to murder his son and says, "Abraham, do not lay your hand on the boy or do anything to him; for now I know that you fear God, since you have not withheld your son, your only son, from me." Abraham then looks around and finds a ram trapped by its horns in a thicket, and he sacrifices that animal in Isaac's place. In the New Testament letter of Paul of Tarsus to the Romans, Chapter 6, Paul is in the midst of his argument about salvation and grace. "For sin will have no dominion over you, since you are not under law but under grace. . . . Now that you have been freed from sin and enslaved to God, the advantage you get is sanctification. The end is eternal life. For the wages of sin is death, but the free gift of God is eternal life in Christ Jesus our Lord." (Rom. 6:14; 22-23.) This is the "ransom theory of the

---

[59]*See* Fox, *Original Blessing*.

[60]Priests for Equality, *The Inclusive Hebrew Scriptures*, 245.

197

atonement," which means that Jesus died in order to redeem humanity. This theology is further illustrated in John 3:16-21, and Revelation 5:12.

> For God so loved the world that he gave his only Son, so that everyone who believes in him may not perish but may have eternal life . . . Those who believe in him are not condemned; but those who do not believe are condemned already, because they have not believed in the name of the only Son of God. . . .Worthy is the Lamb that was slaughtered to receive power and wealth and wisdom and might and honor and glory and blessing!

The pairing of the Abraham/Isaac "text of terror" with these passages is no accident. This ransom theology is embedded in the Christian sacrament of Communion. Christian Eucharist is interpreted as the commemoration of Jesus's last supper with his disciples, where he told them he would be betrayed by them and would go to his death on their behalf. Christianity has made a high ceremony out of it, even a magical working known as "transubstantiation" in which the bread and wine are believed to become literally the flesh and blood of Jesus as the priest celebrates the Mass. To spill the wine or drop the Host then becomes a sacrilege. Literal misinterpretation has resulted in psychic, spiritual, and physical abuse, not to mention accusations of cannibalism.

Holy Communion has been used as a kind of litmus test since the Inquisition of the thirteenth through fifteenth centuries, and recently, during the 2004 U.S. presidential campaign, when American Catholics were warned by some bishops that if they support abortion rights, they are not only out of step with church teaching, but living in a state of sin, and so Communion, which for Catholics is the ultimate symbol of their membership in the realm of God, is denied them. The original argument about grace put forward by the apostle Paul is overthrown in the name of political, social, and personal control of people by fear.

The Eucharist is at the heart of the Christian liturgy. But Matthew Fox proposes that far from being a commemoration of salvation from a state of sin, or a means of control and oppression of the people by the institutional church,

> The Eucharist is about the universe loving us unconditionally still one more time and giving itself to us in the most intimate way (as food and drink). . . The Eucharist is heart food from the cosmos – the "mystical body of Christ" and the Cosmic Christ or Buddha nature found in all beings in the universe – to us. Christ is the light of the world, which we now know is made only of light. Flesh is light and light is flesh. We eat, drink, sleep, breathe, and love that light. The Eucharist is also our hearts expanding and responding generously: "Yes, we will." We will carry on the heart-work called compassion, the work of the cosmos itself.[61]

When we look to what we know about the universe today as a revelation of the nature of God/dess-Creator, Eucharist becomes a sacrament of thanksgiving, celebration, and commitment as we move through the Wheel of the Year. Rather than fall/redemption, or ransom, Eucharist becomes Wisdom's Feast, The Willing Sacrifice, and Sacred Marriage.

Wisdom's Feast

Postmodern people know there is no separate Grandfather Almighty God out there watching over us. We know that good and bad things happen, and we reject the idea that God somehow intervenes with good for some and bad for others. Yet we still are unwilling to abandon the teachings of Jesus that the realm of God is all around us if we just use our eyes and ears and look and listen. Anglican Bishop John Shelby Spong calls those postmodern people *Exiles*[62] for whom traditional church teachings no longer seem relevant to postmodern experience.

In *The Universe Story*, Brian Swimme and Thomas Berry illustrate how new millennium physics teaches that one aspect of the nature of the Universe is relationship:

---

[61]Fox, *Sins of the Spirit,* 271.

[62]Spong, *Why Christianity Must Change.*

Without a sensitivity to primordial communication within the universe, the universe's story comes to an end. That this is certainly the case with an individual organism we can readily appreciate in the case of the monarch butterfly. Climbing out of the pupal shell, stretching its wings in the drying sunlight, what other than the voices of the universe can that butterfly rely upon for guidance? It must make a journey that will cover territory filled with both dangers and possibilities, none of which has ever been experienced before. To rely on its own personal experience or knowledge would be a disaster for the butterfly. Instead it finds itself surrounded by voices of the past, of the other insects, of the wind and the rain and the leaves of the trees.

The information of the genetic material comes forth precisely within its interactions. That is, the monarch butterfly has little if any individual awareness of the difference between beneficial winds and dangerous winds until it finds itself confronted by them in reality. The winds speak to the butterfly, the taste of the water speaks to the butterfly, the shape of the leaf speaks to the butterfly and offers a guidance that resonates with the wisdom coded into the butterfly's being. Such communication takes place beneath the level of language, even that of genetic language. It functions at the primordial reality of primal contact. The source of the guidance is both within and without . . . .[63]

The butterfly is not an *exile*. The butterfly lives in a seamless realm, a matrix, poetically in the palm of God/dess's hand, not alien or estranged. What kind of liturgy, or worship experience, would celebrate the kind of inclusive, nurturing community the butterfly knows without thinking about it?

---

[63]Swimme and Berry, *The Universe Story*, 42.

Even though Communion has been the defining act of worship for Christians, the word "Communion" means a common experience, a common thought, as well as a shared meal. Our most important celebrations are based on sharing food or drink. Eating is one of our most intimate activities, and is rendered sacred in feasts such as Thanksgiving, birthday parties, honorary banquets, or holiday meals. The Olive Garden chain of restaurants advertises that "when you're here, you're family," and the commercials always show an extended family from great-grandfather down to the baby, passing food and drink among themselves in a ritual celebration. Many spiritual traditions include a shared meal, or cup of welcome, an extension of hospitality to the stranger, a commemoration of common experience. Pagan ritual ends with shared cakes and wine.

Eucharist at its root means to give thanks. Just like the monarch butterfly, who finds its way home every year by listening to the elements of the world in which it lives, or like the salmon, that returns from the sea every year, climbs the waterfalls, and lays its eggs in the rivers where the next generation continues the cycle, we can think of ourselves in connection to the universe in the same way. Fox says, "Interconnectivity is the heart of the Eucharistic experience: God and humanity coming together, God and flesh, the flesh of wheat, wine, sunshine, soil, water, human ingenuity, stars, supernovas, galaxies, storms, fireballs – every Eucharist has a 15-billion-year sacred story that renders it holy."[64]

Liturgy brings the people together to consider our place in the universe, to celebrate or commemorate our lives together, to become clear what our purpose is as a community, to strengthen ourselves for the task at hand, and to send ourselves out to continue our common work, transformed and in solidarity. A shared meal using symbols of our shared lives and work is a powerful act. For example, the shared Passover Seder celebrated by Jews every year is commemoration of not only their original liberation from captivity in Egypt, but their continued liberation and their vision of returning to celebrate

---

[64]Ibid.

Passover – *Next Year in Jerusalem.* It is a call to Exiles to remembrance and hope. It is not called "Communion," but that is what it is.

The following words from the prophet Isaiah and from the Wisdom literature of the Jewish tradition are an invitation to *Wisdom's Feast*, to Communion: To celebration of the certainty of God's love and protection – exactly what the Butterfly experiences as it finds its way to its breeding grounds high in the mountains of Colorado.

> Ho! Everyone who thirsts, come to the waters; and those who have no money, come, buy and eat! Come, buy wine and milk without price, for our God calls us away from oppression and greed to a realm of justice and love [pour wine].
> God calls us away from famine and poverty to an abundance of milk and honey [pour milk].
> Wisdom orders all things well: First the grain, then the ear, then the full grain in the ear [break bread].
> To inherit Wisdom is as sweet as the honeycomb [hold up a bowl of honey].
> Wisdom has set her table. She calls from the highest places, "Come, eat of my bread and drink of the wine I have mixed. Come, for all has been made ready."
> [All are invited to come to the table, dip bread into milk, honey or wine. Take as many pieces of bread as is desired. Some may wish to feed one another.

The Willing Sacrifice

The basic premise or developmental theory Karen Armstrong uses in *The Battle for God* is the relationship in human intellect or consciousness between Mythos and Logos – or the relationship between mystic revelation about the meaning of life, and the scientific explanation of the nature of the universe discovered through the reason of the mind. In premodern times, the stories told about the meaning of human life – Mythos – was *understood* to be metaphor; and our human ability to experience the physical realities of the world – Logos – was in balance with Mythos, so that seedtime and harvest, life, death, and rebirth, had meaning. Premodern people were clear about the distinction between myth and physical reality. This is why we have stories about people who slip into Faery accidentally, like Rumpelstiltskin, or legends about how the veil between the worlds is thin in particular times or places. As human consciousness has evolved, and more of the universe has been scientifically understood, the balance has changed between Mythos and Logos, or emotion and reason. By the seventeenth century, reason held sway to such an extent that religious thinkers of the day wanted to be considered just as rational as the scientists, and so they insisted that the old religious myths, like the myth of creation in the Western world, were literally and rationally true. The problem is that once myth becomes literalized, it becomes unbelievable. A lot of unbelievable religious Christian myth was overthrown by Martin Luther and other founders of Protestant religion in the sixteenth and seventeenth centuries. The ultimate result of this predominance of reason was the theology of the transcendence, remoteness, and even the death of God.

In the postmodern period where we are now, there is a movement toward rebalancing mythos and logos, to re-mythologize, or re-enchant the world in which we live. The spiritual task for today's world is to live in the metaphor without making it literal.

As the Wheel of the Year turns, we are constantly reminded of the cycle of birth, life, death, and rebirth – of the cycle of seed transforming into plant, transforming into fruit that sustains life. What gets forgotten or ignored in traditional Christian interpretations of harvest celebrations is the metaphor of sacrifice as a natural part of life. In the language of myth, the young Green Man God of the Beltane seedtime matures into the Sun King God of the Summer Solstice, and becomes in turn the sacrificed God of the harvest – John Barleycorn – who gives up his life so that the land will bring forth food and the people will prosper. As the life of the Sun God wanes toward winter, the life of the consort Goddess of the Moon waxes. Her light provides for the harvest work to continue well into the night so that every last bit of sustenance can be gleaned from the earth. Then at the Winter Solstice, the Goddess nurtures the seed of the next Sun King, and brings forth the Child at Spring: Imbolc

– about February 2 – which is the time of the first births among the animals: – the deer, the cattle, the sheep – and the cycle begins again.

It is normal and natural for humans living close to the earth, who are dependent on the cycles of the seasons, to have invented this great metaphor of the Wheel of the Year. Most of us in the technological world of today have lost track of this. Many of us don't even know the scientific facts of the solstices and the equinoxes, let alone the cross-quarter days that herald the changes in seasons. We look forward to summer's heat, so long as it's not too hot. If it is, we make sure we keep our climate-control devices in good working order. We look forward to Winter and skiing and Christmas, and if we're lucky to have a fireplace, we can enjoy the romance of a fire, and if we really don't like the dirt and effort of chopping and hauling wood, we can switch on a gas fire.

The meaning of the dying-rising God of the seasons who sacrifices life for life has been long lost to us, and in fact that metaphor has been corrupted by theologies of dominion and original sin. Sacrifice in the context of original sin means blood required in expiation or payment. But sacrifice means to make sacred, to make holy. Sacrifice as giving life for life willingly, without thought, is actually at the heart of the nature of the universe in which we have evolved.

In the chapter titled *Supernovas*, from *The Universe Story*, by Brian Swimme and Thomas Berry, the Willing Sacrifice is seen as cosmic metaphor:

> Eventually, in a million years or in several billion years, each star's resources . . . are all used up. If the mass of a star at this point is large enough, its gravitational pressures will destroy the star. The remaining materials will rush toward each other. Nothing in the universe can now stop them. All remaining structure is destroyed as the star implodes to a pulsar – a super-dense mass of neutrons – or [it] collapses all the way down to a naught entity, a singularity of space and time, a black hole. . . .

And yet in the great violent collapse of the star there is a surprising twist of events: the supernova. Not everything is pulled into the nothingness of the pulsar or the black hole. The neutrinos, those wispy and seemingly unimportant elementary particles, escape the collapse. As the star implodes, the neutrinos rush out in all directions to blow off the outer layers of the star, which contain the carbon and oxygen and nitrogen and other elements. Freed from the gravitational death of the star, these elements journey into the night sky, eventually to be drawn together with other elements. Under their own attraction, they form an entirely new system. A new star forms, new planets form, new life forms, and perhaps new consciousness forms; certainly a new area of the story of the universe begins out of the supernova explosion that destroys the old stellar world. . . .[65]

This awesome cycle repeats throughout the universe, and down to the microcosm of our gardens or our window boxes where we might grow a tomato plant or two, and it is incorporated into the mythos of our lives through the examples of the life of Buddha, or the death of Jesus. But we are easily overwhelmed by the enormity of such sacrifice. Christianity especially teaches us humility that takes the form of despair that we can ever live up to such a model. We search for meaning in the notion of finding the "Christ within us," and are convinced that our everyday lives can't possibly include that "Christ consciousness," which was willing to suffer death on a cross for that very impossibility.

In his discussion of "Shadow, Trickster, and Willing Sacrifice,"[66] Unitarian Universalist Rev. Dr. Jeremy Taylor points out that the Willing Sacrifice is an archetype that lives within each of our lives at the most mundane levels. Whenever any growth or change happens in conscious life, the old way

---

[65]Swimme and Berry, *The Universe Story*, 60-61.
[66]Taylor, *The Living Labyrinth*, 256-260.

perforce dies to the new. In the dream world that Taylor writes about, the image of death becomes not physical death, but change – and while change can be and often is individually profound, *any* change at any level is actually the willing sacrifice of the old for the new. Taylor says that even the act of wondering about change, or pausing upon waking to ponder the meaning of a dream is the Willing Sacrifice archetype at work.

But those fantastic examples of the Christ or the Buddha overshadow the microcosmic changes in individual lives. While great moments of willing sacrifice are meant to be inspirational, the result is that most people avoid taking part in these moments at all costs. "For this reason, the mundane tasks of living are all too often, by definition, 'not spiritual.'" So the willing sacrifice of countless millions of women who deny their own need for creativity and personal self-actualization on behalf of their husbands, children, families, communities is unacknowledged, and indeed adds even more sacrifice as women become invisible in terms of who individual women may actually be. The same point applies to the willing sacrifice of countless millions of men equally trapped by the demands of patriarchal obligation to continue the family heritage, to continue the family business, to provide, protect, and defend.

> All these acts, from the most spectacular example of religiously motivated martyrdom and offering up one's best energies for the benefit of others, down to the most mundane gamble – risking a new behavior in the hopes of winning a little more time, a little more love, a little more insight – all embody and exemplify the archetype of Willing Sacrifice. For that reason, they all provide real, concrete occasions for old consciousness and self-awareness to "die" and be renewed, deepened, and expanded, and for broader and deeper realms of consciousness and self-awareness to be "born."[67]

The ritual act that will illustrate for us our role, our part, how we fit into or align with the power of this sacrificial life,

---

[67]Ibid.

death, and rebirth is in the celebration of breaking bread together. The act of taking the bread made from the first grains of the harvest, breaking it, and sharing it among ourselves; and the act of pouring out the libation of wine from the first grapes of the harvest and sharing that among ourselves, can put us in touch with that vast ongoing process. We may call this ritual a Eucharist, a thanksgiving, for the universe loving us unconditionally, and giving itself to us yet again. And we also give of ourselves to one another, and by doing so, we participate in the cosmic metaphor of the willing sacrifice, which we understand to be justice-compassion.

ONE: From the sun to the land, from the land to the stalk, from the stalk to the grain, from the grain to this bread, I consecrate this food in the name of Creator God/dess.

ALL: May their blessings shower upon us through eternity. So mote it be.

ONE: From the moon to the land, from the land to the vine, from the vine to the berry, from the berry to the juice, I consecrate this drink in the name of the Creator God/dess

ALL: May their blessings shower upon us through eternity. So mote it be.

Sacred Marriage

In order to include the metaphor of Sacred Marriage in a ritual Eucharist, it needs to be understood in a much wider context than simply the sexual union of a man and a woman in order to produce children. It needs to be understood at a cosmic level, as it was of old and in the context of our present-day new cosmology, rather than the cosmology of the ancient world. In that world, the Goddess, the Great Mother, brought forth all life parthenogenetically – i.e., without the benefit of input from the God. Later, when humans had figured out the role of sun and seed, the metaphor of sacred marriage was ritualized in the ceremonial union of the king or ruler with the representative of the Goddess in the Temple. Such a ceremony assured the strength, the fertility, the success, the safety of the land and the people. This ceremony is called "temple prostitution" by most clergy, which tinges it with degradation and evil – but that is merely the gloss of 1,600 years of Church dogma. The union of the sun god and the earth goddess, or the Sky with the Earth, is as old as humankind and as varied in interpretation as all the tribes.

For example, the Old Testament Song of Solomon, used traditionally in marriage ceremonies, is actually sacred marriage liturgy from a Mesopotamian ritual reenacting the sexual union of two deities: the fertility god Dummuzi-Tammuz, represented by the king, and his sister Inanna-Astarte, represented by a priestess. The ritual assured fertility of land and people for the coming year. In these sophisticated times, we have little need for that kind of sympathetic magic, at least in a literal sense. But our premodern ancestors knew very well they were dealing with metaphor (mythos) and not with literal truth. They knew they were journeying between the worlds of dream time and waking time. This passionate hymn to sex and abundance would never have been included in the canon if its pagan origins had not been transformed into religious allegory, first recounting God's love for Israel and the history of that relationship, and then reinterpreted as an allegory of Christ's love for the church.

Only four hundred years have elapsed since early in the sixteenth century when Copernicus showed us that the earth is not the center of the universe – and for probably two hundred fifty of those four hundred years, the knowledge has only been available to the rich and educated. No wonder theology has such a hard time breaking out of tradition. Even today, although we now know that there are billions and billions of galaxies and stars and planets, and incredible mysteries of dark matter, black holes, and the theory of creation itself, we are still limited in our perception because we are earth-bound.

Here is Genesis as told with the understanding of the new cosmology:

> At the base of the serene tropical rainforest sits this cosmic hurricane. At the base of the seaweed's column of time is the trillion-degree blast that begins everything. All that exists in the universe traces back to this exotic, ungraspable

seed event, a microcosmic grain, a reality layered with the power to fling a hundred billion galaxies through vast chasms in a flight that has lasted fifteen billion years. The nature of the universe today and of every being in existence is integrally related to the nature of this primordial Flaring Forth. The universe is a single multiform development in which each event is woven together with all others in the fabric of the space-time continuum.[68]

What we need, in Swimme and Berry's words, is a "ritual rapport with the cosmological order and the mythic powers of the universe" as we understand those powers today. There are many ways of relating to or bonding with each other. Our society is in a legal and liturgical debate about what constitutes "marriage." We speak of same-sex unions, partnerships, common-law marriage, single non-celibacy, extended families, how it takes a village to raise a child – yet the very nature of our creativity is a sacred marriage between inspiration and expression.

Sacred Marriage Feast

ONE: Ho, everyone who thirsts, come to the waters; and those who have no money, come, buy and eat! Come, buy wine and milk without price, for our God calls us away from oppression and greed to a realm of justice and love; God calls us away from famine and poverty to an abundance of milk and honey.

ALL: Arise my love, my fair one, and come away; for now the winter is past, the rain is over and gone. The flowers appear on the earth; the time of singing has come, and the voice of the turtledove is heard in our land.

ONE: [Pour wine into a cup] Feasts are made for laughter; wine gladdens our hearts;

ALL: Do not stir up or awaken love until it is ready.

---

[68]Swimme and Berry, *The Universe Story*, 21.

ONE: From the beginning, the alchemy of the universe has provided for life on Earth in due season. [Pour milk into a cup] Milk: the Mother's nurturing food.

ALL: Do not stir up or awaken love until it is ready.

ONE: [Pour honey into a bowl] Honey: the product of Sacred Community.

ALL: Do not stir up or awaken love until it is ready.

ONE: [Break the bread] From the beginning, the guiding myth of the universe has been profligate abundance and willing sacrifice.

ALL: Love is strong as death, passion fierce as the grave.

ONE: Come to the garden, sisters and lovers. Gather myrrh with spice, eat the honeycomb with the honey, drink the wine with the milk. Eat, friends, drink, and be drunk with love.

[All are invited to come and partake of the elements on the table: tear off portions of the bread to dip into the honey; pass the common cups of wine and milk. Some participants may wish to feed each other.]

ALL: Praise and thanks be to the word, and the knowledge, and the wisdom of God, without which nothing was made that was made. All honor and glory and power and blessing be to you, now and forever, worlds without end. Amen.

APPENDIX TWO

Holy Week:
An Exploration of the Meaning of Kenosis

Introduction

Throughout Holy Week, the *Revised Common Lectionary* readings for all three years focus on the Gospel of John, and the Servant Songs of Isaiah. The readings are carefully selected to show that Jesus is God's Son, the Anointed One, known and ordained by God from the beginning of time to suffer and die for the sins of humanity, as foretold by the prophet Isaiah. The writer of John's Gospel intensifies his proof that Jesus is the Christ, the Anointed One, the eternal Logos, the Word of God known from the beginning of time, and the light of the world.

This Holy Week series assumes particular answers to the four questions for the apocalypse, explored in this first volume of commentary on the RCL:

    1) What is the nature of God? Violent or non-violent?

    2) What is the nature of Jesus's message? Inclusive or exclusive?

    3) What is faith? Literal belief, or trust and commitment to the great work of distributive justice-compassion?

    4) What is deliverance? Salvation from hell, or liberation from injustice?

"God" here is non-theistic and "kenotic." *Kenosis* classically means "emptiness." As a Christian term it has been defined as in Philippians 2:6-7: ". . . although [the Anointed One] was born in the image of God, [he] did not regard 'being like God' as something to use for his own advantage, but rid himself of such vain pretension and accepted a servant's lot. . . . [H]e was born like all human beings. . . ."[69] In John Dominic Crossan's words, a *kenotic* god is "the beating heart of the Universe, whose presence is justice and life, and whose absence is injustice and death."[70] Here, *kenosis* includes the desire of a relational spirit for an exiled people to live in justice-compassion. The *kenotic* servant listens and continues to teach reconciliation with that spirit and distributive justice among the people. In these commentaries, *kenotic* "god"

---

[69] Arthur J. Dewey, *et al., The Authentic Letters of Paul,* 186.

[70] Crossan and Reed, *In Search of Paul,* 288-291.

becomes interchangeable with *kenotic* "servant," as the creative force that both contains and is contained by the universe.

In answer to the four questions, the nature of that force is nonviolent; Jesus's message is inclusive, faith is trust in an inclusive, non-violent universe, and deliverance is liberation from injustice. The context for human personal, social, and political life then becomes a covenant with justice and life, and commitment to the ongoing struggle for liberation from injustice.

Civilization defines justice as retribution – payback; an eye for an eye. But the deeper meaning of justice is fair distribution. "Distributive justice" usually is narrowly defined as the fair distribution of wealth. But here the meaning is both wider and deeper, to include the fair distribution of justice. Far beyond economics, as the rain falls on the good, the bad, and the ugly without partiality, distributive justice shows no partiality for any particular human condition. Human civilizations have not used that definition except in cases where there is clearly injustice if partiality enters the picture. The classic example in the United States is that if you are rich, white, and male your chances of serving jail time for possessing cocaine are significantly less than if you are poor, black, and female, charged with possessing marijuana. Occasionally there is a reversal of this pattern, as when an over-zealous North Carolina prosecutor trumped up a case of gang rape of a black stripper against a championship team of white Lacrosse players. In either case, distributive justice is at work – although in a negative sense.

The positive understanding of distributive justice is contained in the term *distributive justice-compassion.* The normal development of civilizations has historically led to systems for assuring safety and security of citizens. But as any reader of Charles Dickens must be aware, those systems often exclude the poor, the uneducated, those who are presumed to have no economic or social power (women, minorities). Members of societies who are denied access to those powers often become ensnared in activities deemed anti-social or criminal in order to survive. Distributive justice-compassion would not demand payback or retribution for such activities, but

214

would provide solutions: reeducation, rehabilitation, redress of grievances. Distributive justice-compassion holds sway in the covenant relationship with the non-violent, inclusive, *kenotic* realm or Kingdom of God. Justice as retribution/pay-back holds sway in the normal march of humanity into civilization. The short-hand term for the seemingly inevitable systems of injustice that are the result of that march is "Empire."[71]

The context for the above four questions for the apocalypse is the postmodern era of the late twentieth and early twenty-first centuries. Generally, historians speak about time in terms of premodern, modern, and postmodern. Premodern refers to the time before the Enlightenment and Descartes. The modern era (post-Enlightenment) lasted for about 350 years. During that time, God was a separate being or entity who created the universe, and proclaimed humanity to be the fulfillment of God's creativity. The "postmodern" era might be argued to have actually begun with Charles Darwin. But regardless of the timing, "postmodern" means the time in which humanity began and continues to deal with the nature of the universe as science has defined it. "God" as a separate being who intervenes in human life from "heaven" somewhere beyond Antares no longer makes intellectual sense.

This leads to another term that has migrated from postmodern science into post-modern spiritual and religious language. In common usage, "cosmology" means the science or theory of the universe. But the term as used by Rev. Dr. Matthew Fox in his ground-breaking theology of original blessing[72] goes beyond the scientific. Cosmology for Fox means humanity's intellectual understanding of the nature of the universe. "Cosmology," as Fox (and this writer, among others) uses the term, describes the mind-set of premodern, modern, and postmodern people, as each of these evolutions of human thought has understood our place in and our relationship to the

---

[71] See especially the work of Jesus Seminar scholars John Dominic Crossan and Marcus J. Borg for a thorough discussion of these concepts.

[72] *See, e.g.*, Fox's *Original Blessing* (Bear & Co., 1983); *The Coming of the Cosmic Christ* (Harper SanFrancisco, 1988).

universe and to God. If, as John Shelby Spong argues, Christianity is to have any relevance at all to postmodern spirituality, changes in focus and metaphor must be made.

Two choices arise from the answers to the four questions that frame this discussion. If the answers are Violent, Exclusive, Literal belief, and Salvation from Hell, then the context for personal, social, and political life becomes the systems of retributive justice that define empire. If the answers are Non-violent, Inclusive, Trust, and Liberation, then the context for personal, social, and political life is covenant with a *kenotic* god: a mutual participation in the ongoing work (struggle) for distributive justice-compassion. The choice for most of human history – including Christian history – has been empire. This series of essays for Holy Week calls for a change in paradigm, and points toward a beginning.

Palm Sunday

Luke 19:28-40; Luke 22:14-23:56; Isaiah 50:4-9a;
Philippians 2:5-11

Palm Sunday is also known as "passion Sunday." The minister has the choice of concentrating on Jesus's triumphal entrance into Jerusalem, hailed as a conquering hero by the fickle crowds (the "Liturgy of the Palms"), or telling the entire "passion" story. The Abingdon Press edition of the RCL admonishes worship planners that "whenever possible, the whole passion narrative should be read." As a result, the liturgy on Palm Sunday can run the dizzying gamut from adulatory parade to Pilate's death sentence in an hour.

In Year C, the RCL offers for consideration Luke's descriptions of Jesus's entry into Jerusalem and Pilate's decision to grant the demand of the crowd and sentence Jesus to death, along with a portion of Paul's letter to the Philippians. The traditional view of both the Jerusalem procession and Philippians 2:9-11 is that this is the imperial Christ triumphant. "Therefore God highly exalted him and gave him the name that is above every name, so that at the name of Jesus every knee should bend in heaven and on earth and under the earth, and every tongue confess that Jesus Christ is Lord."[73]

Marcus J. Borg and John Dominic Crossan suggest that Jesus's "entrance into Jerusalem" on a donkey during the festival of Passover is a parody of Pilate's procession into the city at the same time. Jesus's "peasant procession" came from the east, down the Mount of Olives. Pilate's "military procession" came from the west, in a show of force for law and order.[74] While they base their study on the Gospel of Mark, Luke's Gospel uses Mark, but adds details. A very telling detail – never read if the RCL is followed – is Jesus weeping over the consequences that will arise because of the inability of the people to recognize their visitation from God and the "things

---

[73]Unless otherwise noted, all quotations from scripture are from the New Revised Standard Version (NRSV).

[74]See Borg and Crossan, *The Last Week*.

that make for peace" (Luke 19:41-44). The Palm Sunday parade is a political protest. If Borg and Crossan are also correct in their theory that Luke's birth story was meant as a counter to the birth stories told about Caesar Augustus[75] then Luke's gospel appears to be threaded (albeit subtly) with subversive imagery.

In addition, as these commentaries have suggested, based on Jesus Seminar scholarship, Paul's theology is not one of domination, but of transformation; not of violence and political victory, but of non-violent justice-compassion. Despite the use to which these verses in Philippians 2:9-11 have been put throughout Christian history, the Apostle Paul was not establishing Jesus as the new commander-in-chief of the military might of the known and unknown universe. The hymn was probably not written by Paul. Instead it is probably one of the earliest used by followers of Jesus's Way, and quoted by Paul. The portion of the hymn to the Christ that Paul quotes may be seen to fulfill Isaiah's expectation of deliverance from injustice. It is an ecstatic, mystical declaration that the Emperors of Rome, living and dead, who declared themselves and their ancestors to be "god" and "son of god" and even "very god of very gods" would have to acknowledge that Jesus's name was above even theirs. Jesus was the one chosen by God to be the one to restore God's distributive justice-compassion, in place of the Emperor's retributive justice. In place of law, the Christ establishes radical fairness. The servant of God gives up the power associated with the usual systems of imperial civilization (See Luke 4:1-13). The servant of God is not interested in pay-back or retribution, nor in reward and glorification. The servant of God works with God to establish God's distributive justice-compassion. The servant does the work for the glory of God, and is vindicated, delivered from injustice and death.

Luke's scene where Pilate condemns Jesus to torture and death, along with Philippians 2:7-8 (Jesus "humbled himself and became obedient to the point of death – even death on a cross"), has been interpreted to mean that Jesus agreed to

---

[75]See Borg and Crossan, *The First Christmas*.

submit to the orders of a violently vengeful god and to accept the death penalty on behalf of sinful humanity. Without that payment, humanity cannot be saved from hell. This is the "ransom theory of the atonement." It is the earliest of the atonement theories, probably beginning with the writer of Mark's gospel in the 60s to 70s C.E. Since the twelfth century, St. Anselm's substitutionary atonement has defined the death of Jesus at the hands of the Roman Empire. Mel Gibson's 2004 film, *The Passion of the Christ*, is perhaps the penultimate illustration of that theology. God required that Jesus not only die in our place, but should suffer in order to pay for the sin humanity inherited from Adam and Eve. The greater the sin, the greater the vicarious suffering, the greater Jesus's love for us.

But the first part of the hymn to the Christ is about neither ransom nor substitution. It is about personal *kenosis* – the act of disregarding petty human desires, and defeating the temptation to revel in being the equal of God. "[A]lthough he was born in the image of God, [Jesus] did not regard 'being like God' as something to use for his own advantage, but rid himself of such vain pretension and accepted a servant's lot."[76]

Because Isaiah 50:4-9a is part of the Palm Sunday liturgy, the words of that hymn might be seen as a kind of midrash – a retelling or reframing of that portion of sacred story. As the hymn restates the nature of the ultimate servant of God, the suffering servant described by Isaiah becomes the suffering messiah, who "emptied himself, taking the form of a slave." The servant is obedient to God's law of justice-compassion to the point of death on a cross – the ultimate symbol of imperial law and order. "That is why God raised him higher than anyone and awarded him the title that is above all others . . . ."

Isaiah 50 is not some kind of foretelling of the fate of the future Jesus. It is a model for those who would teach the nature of God. "Morning by morning [God] wakens my ear to listen as those who are taught" sings Isaiah. When we let go of self-interest – ego survival – we "think in the same way that the Anointed, Jesus, did. . . ." We think and act *kenotically* in a constant, evolving struggle of spirit for justice-compassion

---

[76]Dewey, et al., *The Authentic Letters of Paul*, 186.

against the normalcy of civilization. The "suffering servant" trusts God's vindication, that God will prove the servant to be right in the end: "The Lord God has given me the tongue of a teacher, that I may know how to sustain the weary with a word . . . God has opened my ear, and I was not rebellious. . . . I did not hide my face from insult and spitting. . . . Who will declare me guilty? All of them will wear out like a garment."

The cherry–picking of Paul's writings, which are scattered throughout all three years of the RCL, means that the Palm Sunday verses from Philippians are separated from the context in which Paul wrote them. When that happens, Christians can easily ignore or dismiss the action that is called for in 2:1-5, just before the hymn to the Christ. Paul urges the community in Philippi to have this same *kenotic* mind that Jesus had: "regard others as better than yourselves. . . . look not to your own interests, but to the interests of others." With those words, Paul invites the first century Philippians (and anyone in the twenty-first century) to a radical abandonment of self-interest. Paul is talking about creating the realm of God on earth. In such a realm, greed has no place, and debt has no power. Creating such a realm requires the kind of obedience that comes from total commitment to distributive justice-compassion, which can (and often does) lead to death at the hands of imperial systems.

Later in the letter (3:8-9) Paul writes "Indeed, I now regard everything as worthless in light of the incomparable value of realizing that the Anointed, Jesus, is my lord. Because of him I wrote off all of those assets and now regard them as worth no more than rubbish so that I can gain the incomparable asset of the Anointed and be found in solidarity with him, no longer having an integrity of my own making based on performing the requirements of religious law, but now having the integrity endorsed by God, the integrity of an absolute confidence in and reliance upon God like that of the Anointed, Jesus. This integrity is endorsed by God and is based on such unconditional trust in God" (Scholars Version). Here is the meaning of *kenosis* at all levels:

•   a *kenotic* foreign policy – in which crushing debt carried by nations such as Haiti is summarily dismissed;

- *kenotic* business practice – in which profits are secondary to safety, reliability, and sustainability; where debt is not leveraged in order to amass fortunes that seduce others into debt they cannot afford;
- *kenotic* management – in which suggestions for improvement, or whistle-blowing corruption are valued;
- *kenotic* relationships – in which the well-being of the other is foremost.

In the twenty-first century C.E., some are calling for punishment of the speculators and managers who seem to be responsible for the global financial melt-down of 2008-10. Others are holding individual people responsible for making poor choices, or for not having the good sense to avoid the deal that seemed too good to be true. But this is pious revenge. If justice is distributive, there is no need for punishment beyond the consequences already befalling all of us who are caught in the system.

Luke's Jesus weeps over the inability of the people to recognize the coming of the kingdom, and the consequences that will result from that inability. Christians today are too busy getting ready for the Easter Bunny. We don't want to hear how our failure to keep the promises we made during Lent to give up chocolate or stop smoking somehow make us personally responsible for the death of the Son of God two thousand years ago. Somewhere deep in our postmodern brains we know that just isn't true. But what is true is that as soon as we abandon justice-compassion, or ignore the consequences of our actions that lead to unjust systems, we are caught in the powerful currents that propel civilizations into empires.

This is not an indictment of human nature. Empire can happen when people begin to organize themselves into societies, but the good news is that empire is not necessarily inevitable. If we truly turn from our destructive, unjust habits, the old patterns will not be repeated. Sign onto the covenant. Pick up your smart phone and start making sustainable deals that ensure that no part of the interdependent web of life on this planet is compromised. That is the promise and the hope of Palm Sunday.

Blessed is the one who comes in the name of the Lord.

Monday

John 12:1-11; Isaiah 42:1-9; Hebrews 9:11-15

The reading from John's Gospel for Monday of Holy Week revisits the story of the woman with the alabaster jar. The story is so powerful that it appears in all the gospels, and is considered twice by the lectionary readings in Year C. For that reason, some form of this incident may very well have actually happened. The question is when, and under what circumstances. She must have been an important member – even a leader – in Jesus's entourage, even though she is unnamed in Mark, Matthew, and Luke. Mark, Matthew, and John place the story in Jesus's last days as he journeys toward Jerusalem, death, and resurrection. In Luke's version this demonstration was not associated with Jesus's last days. It was an intrusion on a symposium, or banquet, for men only. The woman was a penitent prostitute (by legend, Mary Magdalene), and the story is treated as a scandal. John assumes she was Mary, the sister of Martha and Lazarus, close friends of Jesus. In John's version of the story, "six days before the Passover," there is a dinner for Jesus at the home of Lazarus, whom Jesus has raised from the dead. At this dinner, Lazarus is one of those at table with him, and Martha serves. Mary takes a pound of expensive perfume and anoints Jesus's feet with it, then wipes his feet with her hair.

The RCL includes Hebrews 9:11-15 with the readings for Monday of Holy Week. The writer of Hebrews argues that the Christ came as a high priest from the mysterious order of Melchizedek. This high priest overthrew the old ways of purification through animal sacrifice. "How much more will the blood of Christ, who through the eternal Spirit offered himself without blemish to God, purify our conscience from dead works to worship the living God!" The writer is talking about purity and redemption (buy-back) for transgressions committed under Moses' old covenant. It is because of Jesus's pure blood sacrifice that "those who are called may receive the promised eternal inheritance." These passages – lifted from the context of the full argument – place antisemitism like a faint watermark in the background.

But from Israel's ancient past, Isaiah's "suffering servant" models a different kind of power that brings God's justice-compassion. Whether the servant is a person – perhaps a future king – or represents the collective people of ancient Israel, power is redefined as *kenotic* power. That is, power that is self-denying, not self-aggrandizing. In the first of these "servant songs," the prophet says that the former ways of doing business are well established, but new ways are coming.

> Here is my servant, whom I uphold, my chosen, in whom my soul delights; I have put my spirit upon him; he will bring forth justice to the nations. He will not cry or lift up his voice, or make it heard in the street; a bruised reed he will not break, and a dimly burning wick he will not quench; he will faithfully bring forth justice. He will not grow faint or be crushed until he has established justice in the earth; and the coastlands wait for his teaching.

The mandate is unmistakable: the servant is a partner with God in establishing God's justice, and "the coastlands" – the earth within its coastal boundaries – actively wait – anticipate – look forward to hearing – whatever the servant has to say. Suddenly there is no threat of retributive mayhem or payback, and the universe – perhaps weary of the constant bombardment of human unwillingness to live in trust and wholeness – is waiting for that teaching.

Three times God says that his servant will bring justice, and while it will come with non-violence, and without fanfare, it will come nevertheless with power. How is justice brought forth with power and without violence? Here is where post-modern Christian exiles must part company with the Christian orthodoxy represented by the writer of Hebrews. Jesus death was not a blood sacrifice required to "purify our conscience from dead works to worship the living God." Mary's action at Lazarus' dinner party claims unequivocally that the first part of the prophecy in Isaiah 42 has been fulfilled in Jesus. The meaning of this story is far removed from what is

223

presented in Hebrews. Jesus's death was in the service of God's distributive justice-compassion.

That death – although violent – did not happen in order to bring about God's distributive justice-compassion. That violent death was a result of subverting the old ways of doing business – retributive justice, payback, the usual power structures. Isaiah says that the servant "will bring forth justice to the nations. He will not cry or lift up his voice . . . a bruised reed he will not break, and a dimly burning wick he will not quench; he will faithfully bring forth justice." The poor and those denied access to the usual social and political powers afforded to citizens of civilized societies (the disenfranchised) demand justice because they live with injustice daily. But any human being is susceptible to the corruption of political, social, economic, and personal power systems that lead seemingly inevitably to what John Dominic Crossan calls "the normalcy of civilization." Justice under this "normal" condition is retributive. Power over others and getting even define the only power that seems to make a difference. The rich – the privileged – who control access to the usual expressions of political or social power are the ones most easily corrupted by the power they hold.

This may be the trap Judas found himself in. Mary, Martha, and Lazarus may have been among the rich patrons who supported Jesus. Lazarus sponsored a dinner party for Jesus. Mary may have bought the perfume herself. So what is Judas complaining about? In John's story, Judas is outraged by Mary's extravagant waste of a commodity that could have been sold and the money given to the poor. But it is a false piety. "He said this not because he cared about the poor, but because he was a thief," says John. "He kept the common purse and used to steal what was put into it." The writer was probably setting up Judas for the betrayal to come. The writers of both Luke and John say that the reason Judas betrayed Jesus was that he was possessed by Satan. Without working through the metaphor suggested by this characterization ("the love of money is a root of all kinds of evil" 1 Timothy 6:10), it is possible that after Mary's extravagant misuse of the company funds, the only way Judas could see to ensure his own economic survival was to turn Jesus in to the collaborators with Roman authority.

But money is not what brings God's distributive justice. What brings God's distributive justice is "my servant, whom I uphold, my chosen, in whom my soul delights." Mary uses the money to buy a pound of pure nard, and instead of keeping it "for the day of my burial," as Jesus suggests, she anoints Jesus's feet with it. Jesus says, "You always have the poor with you, but you do not always have me." Money designated by the rich for the poor merely continues to buy into the normal systems that keep injustice and violence in place. Instead of making the expected donation, Mary has acknowledged Jesus as the servant of God, and has anticipated his death.

Tuesday

John 12:20-36; Is. 49:1-7; 1 Corinthians 1:18-31

Light versus darkness, revelation versus secrecy, wisdom versus foolishness are the motifs that are interwoven in the readings for this day. Christian tradition has so intertwined and literalized these metaphors that it is nearly impossible for postmodern exiles to glean any other meaning than what has come to be "orthodox" (correct) belief. The RCL does not follow the sequence of John's narrative. Knowing that John's Gospel was written seventy to ninety years after the death of Jesus, and thirty to fifty years after the fall of Jerusalem and the destruction of the temple hardly helps. As presented by the RCL, John's Gospel bears little if any connection to participation in God's justice-compassion on earth, here and now. Instead, it dazzles and distracts us with promises of becoming "children of light" if we will only believe. The story is not important; conveying the theology and proving the supremacy of Christianity is what matters.

The "servant's songs" in Isaiah are attributed to an unknown prophet who lived in Babylon during the Babylonian exile of the Jewish people during the sixth century, B.C.E. The servant is often interpreted to be the nation of Israel, not an individual, and in this second song (Is. 49:1-7) God declares to the entire earth (bounded by the "coastlands") that the nation of Israel has been called to serve God's justice-compassion. The servant Israel has been hidden away, and even though it looks as though that great work of justice-compassion has gone unnoticed, it has not. God will restore the servant people to power and kings and emperors will stand up and take notice. God says, "I will give you as a light to the nations, that my salvation may reach to the end of the earth." "Salvation" in this context does not mean "going to heaven at death." "Salvation" in terms of the Isaiah of the Babylonian exile means liberation from enemies. In the wider sense of Isaiah 55, it means living in God's kingdom of distributive justice and peace for all of the days allotted to life, whether of the community, or the individual members. The Jesus of the Synoptic Gospels may have pointed to these prophecies as encouragement to his followers, struggling to love justice and live in non-violent resistance to Rome. He is highly unlikely to have claimed that he himself was the fore-ordained embodiment of Isaiah 49, which Christian tradition continues to do.

The readings for holy week from John's gospel do follow their own logic. On Monday, Mary, the sister of Lazarus and Martha, anoints Jesus's body in advance for burial. On Tuesday, John's Jesus delivers his last public dialogue, in which he claims the metaphor of seed and grain, life and light, and God Himself speaks from heaven in response to Jesus's pious invocation: "Father, glorify your name." God thunders that "I have glorified it, and I will glorify it again." And we understand that to mean the glorification of the once and future Christ Jesus. Jesus proclaims that the ruler of this world (Satan) will be driven out, and that Jesus the Christ will be lifted up and "will draw all people to myself. . . While you have the light, believe in the light, so that you may become children of light."

After this, Jesus (the servant) goes into hiding. This is not the first time in John that Jesus has disappeared for some period of time (see 7:1,10; 8:59). Most recently (12:36) after the raising of Lazarus, Caiaphas, the high priest, declares ". . . it is better for you to have one man die for the people than to have the whole nation destroyed." From that time on, John says, "they planned to put Jesus to death." So Jesus "no longer walked about openly among the Jews, but went from there to a town called Ephraim in the region near the wilderness; and he remained there with the disciples."

Jesus does a lot of hiding out in John, and swears everyone to secrecy in Mark. But that is no reason to think that when the prophet says in Isaiah 49:2b "in the shadow of his hand he hid me," the prophet is talking about Jesus. When the prophet says "I will give you as a light to the nations," he is not talking about John's Jesus, who says, when the people ask him who is the Son of Man who will be lifted up, "The light is with you for a little longer. . . While you have the light believe in the light, so that you may become children of light." That is John's insightful metaphor, which may be said to claim that Jesus is the fulfillment of the servant song. But in order to fulfill that

227

prophecy, the servant must suffer the consequences of countering the political powers that be.

The portion from 1 Corinthians is apparently pivotal to Christian orthodoxy because it is required reading in all three lectionary years: twice in years B and C and three times in year A: Holy Cross (all three years; September 14); Lent 3 (year B); Tuesday of Holy Week (all three years); and 4 Epiphany (year A). But 1 Cor. 18 cannot be taken at face value: "For the message about the cross is foolishness to those who are perishing, but to us who are being saved it is the power of God" (Scholars Version). Taken out of its context, and put together with the other readings understood in the traditional way, this verse is arrogant, exclusive, and – given its association with verse 23b – antisemitic. Paul's opening salvo needs to be studied in its whole context, from 1:10 through 2:17. Two points made by Crossan and Reed need to be kept in mind. First, Paul's theology sets the Realm/Kingdom of God in opposition to the empire of Rome. Second, Paul's theology contrasts the self-serving normalcy of civilized life with the radical denial of self-interest *(kenosis)* of those who are committed to the great work of restoring God's distributive justice-compassion. When these two points are understood, antisemitism disappears, along with Christian spiritual exclusivity and Christian political hegemony.

So, Paul is blasting his friends in Corinth for fighting about which baptism carries the most weight. Paul says he wishes he hadn't baptized anyone, because Christ did not send him to baptize people but to proclaim the power of the cross of Christ. That power, says Paul, makes no sense to those who are "perishing" by living according to the unjust systems of Roman imperial society. But those who get the point of the crucifixion of Jesus are liberated from injustice, and empowered to join and continue the work. Paul calls for the Corinthians to consider who they were when they joined the group. "Not many of you" were powerful or of noble birth – which implies that some indeed were. But those who were of high rank or social status don't get to brag about that, and claim power over others in the community. "Let the one who boasts boast in the Lord," Paul says.

Twenty-first century Christian leaders must repudiate the emphasis on Paul's phrase, "we proclaim Christ crucified, a stumbling block for Jews and foolishness to Gentiles." Clearly, this phrase has been used in the service of antisemitism from the beginning of the organized Christian Church. Further, "Gentiles" has often meant non-Christians other than Jews who do not believe the Christian myth. Both interpretations have been and continue to be anachronisms because the phrase has been lifted out of its context. Paul goes on to say that "to those who are called, both Jews and Greeks, Christ [is] the power of God and the wisdom of God." In other words, to those who agree to participate in the restoration of God's realm of distributive justice-compassion, regardless of who they may be, the crucified Christ symbolizes the power and the wisdom of God's *kenotic* action in the world.

Because Paul was a devout Jew, and a Pharisee, he uses Jewish theology to powerful effect. One aspect of Jewish theological tradition is the concept of the Wisdom of God. Wisdom is personified as the feminine spirit who was with God from the beginning, who pitched her tents among the people, who calls from the heights beside the way. When Paul says that "Christ [is] the power and the wisdom of God," he is drawing on ancient and revered Jewish tradition. In 1 Corinthians 2:8, he says "Yet among the mature we do speak wisdom . . . But we speak God's wisdom, secret and hidden, which God decreed before the ages for our glory." "Lay aside immaturity," Wisdom says, "and live and walk in the way of insight" (Proverbs 9:6; *see, especially,* Proverbs 8).

God's wisdom is revealed through God's *kenotic,* radically self-denying spirit, which was embodied in Jesus. When Jesus died, that same spirit was then extended to those who can accept it. This is craziness to people caught up in the normalcy of social hierarchy and control. It is liberation to those who are able to discern that it is spiritual truth. They (we) "have the mind of Christ" – as we were inspired to do by the readings for Palm Sunday. What is revolutionary in these readings is not the magic of believing a story about Jesus. What is revolutionary is that the very nature of power as humanity generally understands it is reversed. The servant is the cornerstone. Relinquishing one's very well-being to the point of death carries more power than any earthly ruler who relies on retributive systems to maintain his or her position. Faith is knowing the truth of that assertion regardless of all evidence to the contrary.

Wednesday

John 13:21-32; Isaiah 50:4-9a; Hebrews 12:1-3; Psalm 70

For those who choose not to do the Passion readings on Palm Sunday, Isaiah 50:4-9a is revisited now, but not in the context of Paul's letter to the Philippians ("at the name of Jesus every knee should bend in heaven and on earth and under the earth, and every tongue confess that Jesus Christ is Lord"). Now the emphasis is on the willingness of the servant to submit to the will of God: "I was not rebellious, I did not turn backward. . . I did not hide my face from insult and spitting." John's Jesus knows who will betray him, and clearly indicates who it is by handing Judas the bread after it has been dipped in the bowl – yet the disciples fail to realize what is right in front of their faces: The hour for Jesus's death, resurrection, and ascension has arrived.

If the readings suggested by the RCL are simply read in the context of traditional Christian belief, the story of the servant depicted in Isaiah easily becomes a prequel to the suffering and death of Jesus, the Messiah. The Psalm then is a plea on the part of listeners to be saved from such a death: "Be pleased, O God, to deliver me . . . Let those be put to shame and confusion who seek my life . . ." The verses cherry-picked from the pastoral letter called "Hebrews" reassure that "since we are surrounded by so great a cloud of witnesses . . ." we can indeed "run with perseverance the race that is set before us . . ." That portion of the sermon by the writer of Hebrews has been used by would-be preachers and genuine prophets of Christianity for nearly two millennia. In his last speech, Dr. Martin Luther King, Jr. made reference to those who did not receive what was promised in their lifetimes, but who, like Moses and King himself, had been to the mountain top and had been privileged to see the promised land. The "cloud of witnesses" refers to a litany of the Judeo-Christian journey (Heb 11:29-40), and the promise of the power of the Christ coming again. But if read beyond the portion selected by the RCL, the metaphor soon breaks down into a thinly-veiled antisemitism along with the usual threats of hell-fire and damnation: ". . . for if they did not escape when they refused the one who warned them on earth, how much less will we escape if we reject the one who warns from heaven! . . . for indeed our God is a consuming fire" (12:25-29)

Because we already know the story from Mark, Matthew, and Luke, we assume that John's Judas has already conspired with the high priest Caiaphas to hand Jesus over to the religious authorities for thirty pieces of silver. We assume that the reason the "chief priests and the Pharisees" in John's story wanted to kill Jesus was because of Jesus's demonstration against the money-changers in the Temple. We never read John 11:45-57, in which the religious authorities plot to kill Jesus. We never learn that Jesus's raising of his friend Lazarus from the dead was the last straw for the high priest Caiaphas. "This man is performing many signs," Caiaphas tells the meeting of the council. "If we let him go on like this, everyone will believe in him, and the Romans will come and destroy both our holy place and our nation." (The Romans did indeed destroy Jerusalem, well before John wrote his gospel, but not because Jesus raised Lazarus from the dead, or performed any other "signs.") John then says, "Jesus therefore no longer walked about openly among the Jews, but went from there to a town called Ephraim in the region near the wilderness; and he remained there with the disciples" until the time came for him to return to Jerusalem for the final Passover. "Now the chief priests and the Pharisees had given orders that anyone who knew where Jesus was should let them know, so that they might arrest him." The stage is set for Judas leading both Roman soldiers and Temple police to arrest Jesus in the garden, not for the exchange of silver or Judas' eventual remorseful suicide.

Judas' motives have been the subject of speculation since the story was first told. Jesus hands the bread to Judas and tells him to "Do quickly what you are going to do," and Judas goes out into the night. John's version of the story says that "Some thought that because Judas had the common purse," Jesus was telling him to buy supplies for their Passover festivities, or make a donation to the poor – acts of easy piety. The writer of John's gospel concludes that Judas was taken over by Satan. In *The Last Week,* Borg and Crossan write that ". . . it is possible to gain control of the earth by demonic collaboration. It is possible to fall prey to the ancient (and modern) delusion of religious power backed by imperial violence"(p. 206). Quite probably, Judas did what he thought was right. He abandoned what had to look like a lost cause in occupied Jerusalem in order to save himself from the consequences of being associated with a man the authorities wanted to arrest. Caiaphas did what he thought he needed to do in order to survive and preserve what he perceived to be the Jewish way of life. Indeed, John has him say that "it is better to have one man die for the people than to have the whole nation destroyed" (John 11:50). Ultimately, Pontius Pilate was absolutely correct in sentencing Jesus to death for the sake of preserving law and order and his own position as the Roman ruler of Palestine.

There is nothing supernatural about Jesus's conviction that he would be turned over to the religious authorities, and likely ultimately executed by the Roman occupiers. Jesus maintains his integrity in the service of justice-compassion, against the normalcy of civilization, relying upon the same kind of faith as Isaiah's servant. But the *kenosis* illustrated by the third servant song of Isaiah is not submission to the will of an interventionist God who wants a sacrifice in payment for sin, or who "disciplines those whom he loves, and chastises every child whom he accepts" (Heb. 12:5-6 *ref* Proverbs 3:11-12). Instead this *kenosis* means actively listening to the desire of a relational spirit for an exiled people to live in justice-compassion. The servant says, "Morning by morning he wakens my ear to listen as those [do] who are taught." The servant listens and continues to teach reconciliation with that spirit and distributive justice among the people. The servant does this despite persecution, torture, failure, and insult. He empowers the people to maintain their covenant with God against the demonic forces that impel the people to collaborate with the empire that has carried them off into exile.

The disciples could not hear what John's Jesus was trying to tell them. The others around the table that night apparently had no clue as to the danger that he (and they) were in because of the threat that he (and they) presented to law and order under Roman occupation. Judas was not the only follower of Jesus to be caught up in the mind-set that reduces teachings of

233

non-violent justice-compassion to empty piety. To live and practice non-violent justice-compassion is to actively counter the imperial forces that seduce us into going shopping, hiring illegal aliens as slave labor, and joining the military because we have been convinced that it is the only way to obtain peace and security and "be all we can be."

The creators of the RCL leave out verses 10 and 11 of Isaiah 50, and they should not because the servant addresses those very conditions that produce empty piety instead of an active counter to imperial retributive systems. The servant wonders "who [among you] walks in darkness and has no light, yet trusts in the name of the Lord and relies upon his God?" The conclusion is, few if any. But in a post-modern world, where for many the interventionist god died long ago, the servant's challenge to faith has meaning only if we accept the invitation to participate in the ongoing great work of justice-compassion. Then we become partners with the *kenotic* servant God in restoring God's justice-compassion to the world – which belongs to that *kenotic* servant God. And the life and death of the servant-teacher Jesus is the model.

Thursday

Exodus 12:1-14; Psalm 116:1-2, 12-10; John 13:1-17; 31b-35;
1ˢᵗ Cor. 11:23-26

Holy Week began with Jesus's demonstration countering the pomp and circumstance of imperial force; Monday was a foreshadowing of the consequences of taking such a stance against the powers and principalities of normal human systems, as Mary anoints Jesus, preparing his body in advance for death. Tuesday provided the theological context. God's wisdom raises the slave above all others who would pretend to be the rulers of the universe. Wednesday suggested Jesus as the model of that *kenotic* servant. This is not a power-over others, but a power-with the seamless matrix of Being in the Universe. On Thursday those who would follow that model receive the mandate. When the Church conflates John's pre-Passover footwashing with the imagery of the Paschal Lamb and the stories of the "last supper" in the synoptic gospels, the result is a mixed metaphor: Forgiveness of "sin" is confused with deliverance from injustice, and the radically inclusive equality of the Kingdom of God is lost.

In John's version of Jesus's story, Jesus "loved his own, who were in the world, [and] he loved them to the end." As a demonstration of that self-less love, Jesus takes off his outer robe, wraps a towel around himself, and proceeds to wash his disciples' feet and dry them with the towel. In the normal course, as the master teacher, Jesus would be justified in expecting that his disciples wash his feet. But Jesus never does what would be expected in the normal course. His *kenotic* action is a demonstration of how his followers are to treat one another. After he has washed their feet he says, "I have set you an example that you also should do as I have done to you . . . I tell you, servants are not greater than their masters, nor are messengers greater than the one who sent them. If you know these things, you are blessed if you do them." In other words, John's Jesus says, if you understand the conventional social arrangement (servants are not greater than their masters), congratulations. But look at what I have just done. The master has become the servant; the order of normal human interaction is reversed. When Peter objects, Jesus says, "Unless I wash you, you have no share [i.e., nothing in common] with me." Taken at face value, these words seem contradictory or exclusionary; instead, they illustrate the profound equality of power in the Kingdom of God.

The inclusion of Exodus 12:1-14 in the list of readings for Maundy Thursday seems to confirm John's theology that Jesus is the new Paschal Lamb. Twice John refers to the day and time of Jesus's death being the "day of preparation" for the Passover, when the Passover lambs were ritually slaughtered in the Temple (see John 19:14; 19:31). But the synoptic tradition does not make that connection. The blood of the Paschal Lamb was smeared above the doors of the ancient Hebrews enslaved in Egypt so that God's angel of death would pass over them. The Paschal Lamb is a symbol of deliverance, both from God's judgment for injustice, and from the people's enemies. It is not a symbol of forgiveness of sin. As John's high priest Caiaphas says (albeit without a clue what he was saying at the time), ". . . it is better for you to have one man die for the people than to have the whole nation destroyed" (John 11:50-52) Jesus is the willing sacrifice – the one who willingly chooses to give up his life in the process of restoring God's justice-compassion to God's world. Borg and Crossan say it best:

> Recall, however, the challenge of Jesus in [Mark] 8:34-35: ". . . those who want to save their life will lose it, and those who lose their life for my sake . . . will save it." Recall also [that] . . . Peter wanted no part of that fate, the Twelve debated their relative worth, and James and John wanted first seats afterward. But Jesus had explained to them quite clearly that his and their life was a flat contradiction to the normalcy of civilization's domination systems. In other words it was by participation with Jesus and, even more, in Jesus that his followers were to pass through death to resurrection, from the

domination life of human normalcy to the servant life of human transcendence.[77]

There is no "institution of the Lord's Supper" in John, and so the RCL offers what is thought to be the original from Paul's first letter to the Corinthians. Paul's Jesus declares, "This cup is the new covenant in my blood. Do this, as often as you drink it, in remembrance of me." Paul explains, "for as often as you eat this bread and drink the cup, you proclaim the Lord's death until he comes." But these words have become identified with substitutionary atonement and apocalyptic second-coming imagery. The Eucharist has become the commemoration of Jesus's betrayal and death, and the confession of sin as complicity on the part of his followers (then and now) in that action. The celebrant proclaims "The blood of the new covenant poured out . . . for the forgiveness of sins." But that is not what Paul intended.

The purpose of the shared meal that became the defining ritual of early Christianity was to renew the covenant with God for radical, distributive justice, and to pledge to keep the covenant until the Christ would come again. Like the foot-washing ritual in John's story, the usual social order was reversed. Instead of a public sacrifice and banquet intended to maintain the proper relationships between the social elements of clients and patrons, extending to the emperor and ultimately to the gods (and to the god Caesar), the bread and cup were a symbol of the absence of hierarchy among the members of the communities founded by Paul (the body of Christ). In the Corinthians passage, which is of course lifted out of context, Paul explains that if the ritual meal maintains the usual social hierarchy, then it is not "the Lord's supper" (1 Cor. 11:17-22).

The Maundy Thursday Tenebrae ritual, whether it includes footwashing, or simply the re-enactment of Jesus's last supper, sends us out of the church in silence and darkness to contemplate our complicity in Judas' betrayal. The betrayal is understood to be the sin that Jesus forgives. But traditional commemorations of the last night Jesus spent with his disciples risk empty if not dangerous piety. Piety is empty when it relies

---

[77]Ibid., 119-120.

on the certainty of forgiveness without accountability and unaccompanied by transformation; piety is dangerous when it is aligned with imperial injustice. Followers of Jesus's Way are complicit with Judas, not because of personal wrongdoing, or some kind of "original sin" dating back to Adam and Eve, and certainly not because of vicarious responsibility for Jesus's death. Followers of Jesus's way are complicit with Judas because it is so much easier to settle for survival. If we try to organize a union where we work in our local grocery store chain, we will be fired. If we preach a twenty-first century faith, based on scholarship and the realities of twenty-first century life, we will be ignored at best or fired and defrocked. If we defend terrorists, our homes may be fire-bombed. If we come out as gay, lesbian, bi-sexual, transgendered humans, our civil rights are curtailed. If we provide legal abortions to poor women, we risk being murdered.

It gets worse. Whether we claim to be followers of Jesus's Way or not, if we invest our money in the companies that give us the best return, we could be supporting companies that exploit workers, intimidate whistle-blowers, and disrupt the balance of the Earth's eco-systems. If we move to the country to escape the stress of the city, we could end up with a much less sustainable life-style, unless we grow our own food. The "interdependent web of which we are a part," celebrated by Unitarian Universalists, is nearly totally compromised by the normalcy of human social systems.

Holy Week, beginning with Palm Sunday, may be a time of profound ritual of remembrance but what is more important is that it is a time for recommitment to the great work of distributive justice-compassion, in the face of the overwhelming strength of conventional, normal, social and political systems. Maundy Thursday, when the mandate to love one another as Jesus loved his disciples is powerfully demonstrated by Jesus, is actually the heart of Holy Week. The execution of Jesus at the hands of Rome is not the point. The belief in the resurrection of Jesus as a verifiable fact is also not the point, no matter how many reinterpretations of the metaphor of the empty tomb. The point is *kenosis*: the radical abandonment of self-interest in the service of distributive justice-compassion, with the expectation that living such a life leads to death on a cross, and the willingness to take that risk.

Tenebrae Eucharist

One: On the last night with his disciples, as they lounged at their dinner, Jesus decided to try one last time to make them really understand what he was doing, and what it really meant to follow him.

Another: He picked up a loaf of bread, and spoke into the hubbub of their conversation: Listen! – he said – This bread is like God's justice in this world. Then he tore the loaf into two pieces. This is God's justice in the hands of the Romans and the Temple authorities who collaborate with them. Believe me, one of you is going to turn me in to them soon. If not tonight, then as soon as the Passover is finished. Whenever you eat together after this night, remember that, and remember me.

One: Then Jesus picked up the jug of wine.

Another: This wine is also like the Kingdom of God – it is the blood of the Paschal Lamb, painted on the lintels and doorposts of our people as a sign that they belong to God and not to Pharoah's Empire. But now the collaborators have made this wine into a corruption – a libation poured out in honor of the Empire of Rome. – a repudiation of God's protection and deliverance.

One: And he poured the wine into a cup and held it up to them.

Another: He said, "Let the one who has chosen this cup take his possessions and do what he must." And he dumped the contents into a bowl for disposal.

One: Several of the company began to leave quietly, and he let them go. Then he poured a second cup of wine and said, "But this cup that I drink is a new cup. It is a libation of my blood poured out for justice for all those who choose to share it. Drink it. All of you who are willing to commit to establish God's justice-compassion, and remember.

240

Another:	He passed the cup to them, and they passed it among themselves as a pledge. And while they were doing this, one of the women – perhaps it was Mary of Magdala – the one who Jesus loved – left the room and returned with a tiny jar of essential oil of lavender. And she came up to Jesus's couch and said, "You will die for what you have done this week – perhaps tonight – and I know I will never have the chance to prepare your body for burial. If they take you, there will be nothing left."
One:	Then she broke open the vial and anointed his face and hands. And he took it from her and went to the one next to him and said, "She has done what she could. She has prepared my body for death. Do the same for one another in remembrance of her." And he anointed that one, and that one went to the next until all in the company had been so ordained.

Friday

John 18:1-19:37; Isaiah 52:13-53:12

John's detailed story of the arrest, crucifixion, and burial of Jesus is intricately interwoven with the third Song of the Suffering Servant in Isaiah. John is especially interested in showing that Jesus died in fulfillment of scripture. Two millennia of tradition, visual art, musical art, and film confirm the basic belief of all Christianity: "Surely he has borne our griefs and carried our sorrows. . . he was wounded for our transgressions . . . and the Lord has laid on him the iniquity of us all." There isn't a choir member on the planet who has not sung these choruses from Handel's great Messiah.

As should be evident from this past week of commentary, this Christology cannot be reclaimed; it must be replaced. Neither guilt nor self-loathing are emotions that empower people to love others, or spur people to take action with justice as radical fairness, or to give up systems that demand retribution and payback. Jesus was not executed by the representatives of the Roman Empire because God needed a scapegoat to carry away the sins of the world. Jesus was executed because the way of life that he taught challenged and contradicted the conventional order. Jesus's Way overturns the normal systems of piety, war, and victory, and restores God's covenant: non-violence, distributive justice, and true peace.

Kenosis, in this series of essays, means the radical abandonment of self-interest in the service of distributive justice-compassion. It is the *kenotic* servant, who actively listens to the desire of a relational spirit for reconciliation with that spirit and distributive justice among the people. The servant empowers the people to maintain their covenant with God despite persecution, torture, failure, and insult from the demonic forces of conventional social systems that insist upon collaboration. When we make that choice, as John's Jesus showed and taught us, we suffer because that choice can mean going against family, friends, church, and society into a kind of exile. Worst of all, seldom do we see any confirmation that our choice has made any difference. The descriptions of Jesus's death in Mark and Matthew are brilliant in their empathic identification with the most profound despair that anyone can experience: abandonment by God. Injustice and death at the hands of unjust systems indicate the absence of the *kenotic* god and the invalidation of covenant. Jesus was not only betrayed and abandoned by his friends; in his experience he was in fact abandoned even by his God.

The question for twenty-first century Christians is not whether you accept Jesus as your Lord and Savior, but whether your Jesus – your Christ – your Lord – your God – is violent, demanding retributive justice, or non-violent, expecting and desiring distributive justice-compassion. The choice we make regarding the nature of our God determines the quality of life for all sentient beings on the planet. The non-violent, non-interventionist, *kenotic* God, without ego, without being, is the context within which and from which the earth and all its creatures realize wholeness. That is the nature of the covenant.

The violent death of anyone, whether working for the cause of justice-compassion or not – signals the refusal of the ruling authorities to be open to the spirit of that *kenotic* god, whose presence is justice and life. Such a death – like the crucifixion and death of Jesus – establishes the violation of covenant, and the absence of God.

Saturday

John 19:38-42; Job 14:1-14

"As waters fail from a lake, and a river wastes away and dries up, so mortals lie down and do not rise again; until the heavens are no more, they will not awake or be roused out of their sleep . . . If mortals die, will they live again? All the days of my service I would wait until my release should come." So the writer of Job – taken out of the context the writer intended – plunges us into the stark reality of the death of the servant, who dies in the service of God's justice, and waits for God's vindication. Holy Saturday is the *via negativa:* the journey into darkness, despair, hopelessness, death.[78]

The developers of the RCL, of course, have cherry-picked the passages from Job, ending with the servant's anticipated release. But if the entire chapter is read, the mourning for loss is profound: If my release should come, the servant Job says, "[God] would call, and I would answer; [God] would long for the work of [God's] hands. . . [God] would not keep watch over my sin . . . But the mountain falls and crumbles away, and the rock is removed from its place . . . so you [God] destroy the hope of mortals . . . their children come to honor and they do not know it; they are brought low, and it goes unnoticed. . . ." By stopping with verse 14, the possibility is left open for the theological argument about how Jesus descended into Hell to release the souls of the martyrs. But as far as Jesus's community of followers was concerned, as of the Sabbath, the powers and principalities had won. It is important to realize how possible such an outcome is in the twenty-first century.

The powers and principalities, the normalcy of civilization, the seemingly inevitable domination of empire and systems of retribution have brought us to the brink of human if not planetary extinction. To quote Borg and Crossan yet again, " . . . we can do it already in about five different ways – atomically, biologically, chemically, demographically, ecologically – and

---

[78]See Fox, *Original Blessing.*

244

we are only up to e."[79] Politically, the United States is the first among equals of violent empire, following the drumbeat of military and economic power in pursuit of world domination.[80] Much of U.S. foreign, domestic, and economic policy is grounded in violent ideology that is deaf to reality, even provable, measurable, physical realities such as global warming, mortal poverty, and ignorance. We should sit in dust and ashes for a moment, and not skip blithely into Easter's happy ending. Without experiencing *via negativa*, without traveling to the middle of the labyrinth, past the demons, we can never arrive at the fire at the center where the creative response is generated, and the key to the way out into transformation is found.

Without death, there is no life. This is the law of the universe.

---

[79]Borg and Crossan, *The Last Week*, 171.

[80]

Whether or not the deliberate intent of U.S. policies, foreign and domestic, is world domination, the result of U.S. hegemony is its identification as the only "super power." While a discussion of this point is beyond the scope of this essay, a colleague has pointed out that "what the United States seems to be obsessed with is not 'world domination,' but the futile search for absolute economic and political security. We need to open ourselves to the transformative understanding that in this complex, interdependent world, peace and prosperity can only be achieved through the creation of justice, not by force." In other words, what is needed is the restoration of Covenant.

Made in the USA
Lexington, KY
02 March 2013